# BROKEN EYES, UNBROKEN SPIRIT

# BROKEN EYES, UNBROKEN SPIRIT

the story of a national
blind golf champion

David Meador

This book is based on true events. Some names and situations were changed at the author's discretion.

Published by David Meador
Nashville, TN
www.davidmeador.com

Published in the United States of America

Cover and interior design: Christa Shoenbrodt, Studio Haus

Meador, David.
     Broken eyes, unbroken spirit: the story of a national blind golf champion.
     ISBN 978-0-9829652-0-7

*To my wife, Connie, who finds joy in the little things.*

*Young David*

# ACKNOWLEDGEMENTS

My sincerest heartfelt thanks to: Mary Helen Clarke, editor of several *New York Times* best sellers, for her invaluable guidance and help during the early years of this eight-year project; my wife Connie, daughter Julia, and her husband Wil for their painstaking edits and loving collaborations of my many "final" drafts; and my daughter Emily for her two children (my grandchildren) and her inspiring example of persistence under difficult circumstances.

# SPECTACULAR CATCH

My story begins in 1964, a time of peace and optimism for most of America. The Beatles were being introduced for the first time to a sprawled-out American teenage audience watching The Ed Sullivan Show. Vietnam had not yet moved into the lead position on the evening news. And even the haunting memory of President Kennedy's assassination months earlier had begun to fade from the present to the past.

On a crisp Saturday morning, Southern Illinois University's football stadium warmed itself under an October sun. Seventy-five miles north, our small town's high school football team boarded a bus. We were on our way to see a real college game.

Swept along in conversation, one bold statement led to another. Before we knew it, five of my friends and I made a decision. We were going to make a name for ourselves. We decided to steal a college football. Not just any ball, but the official ball from the middle of a college game.

The SIU Salukis finally scored a touchdown early in the fourth quarter. The two teams lined up for the extra point. The center hiked. The opposing lines crashed and growled. As soon as the ball left the kicker's foot and lifted toward the uprights, my friends leaped from the back of the end zone and into the game film, much to the surprise of coaches, players, fans, and the two team managers assigned to retrieve that coveted ball.

As the ball fell to the end zone, our third-string halfback, Tony, timed his jump perfectly. He snared the pigskin in mid-air, pivoted, and fired the ball past the Saluki team managers. The ball shot like a bullet to my friend Randy on the far side. Spectators and players stared in disbelief as the bristling managers ran among my teammates, frantically trying to break up our play.

In the mayhem of the moment, Randy saw himself as if he were on TV. My high school buddy caught the ball, reared back, and launched the highest and longest spiral of his life. The hijacked oblong soared up into the sunlit view of the crowd. The ball turned over in mid-flight and nosed down just beyond the stadium's wrought-iron fence into my outstretched arms.

On the parking lot side of the fence, I made an over-the-shoulder catch and sprinted down a steep grassy grade to the standing ovation of stadium fans. Eyes focused on the ground in front of me, I never looked back. I disappeared into lengthening shadows, all the time swiveling hips and fending off imaginary tacklers.

When I looked up, I faced a small ZIP code of parked cars. Grillworks gaped at me with open eyes. It was only at that moment, protecting the ball after the spectacular catch, that I saw an unexpected dilemma: Where could I go from here? I had precious few options. The giant parking lot was surrounded by another tall fence, complete with a guarded front entrance. Should I try to climb that fence? Should I try to sneak past those front sentries with the ball under my jacket?

Crouched between a car and a pickup, I peered around taillights and saw to my dismay the two perturbed team managers power-walking my way. They pounded up the parking lot looking more like Chicago thugs than frat brothers. "Here you go, guys," I said, as I coughed up the ball to the angry managers. To my relief, they took the ball and walked away.

Just a few days later, we read a Southern Illinois community newspaper. Headline: "Salukis Lose Game, Plus Game Ball!" The article went on to say that there was an upside. At least fans saw one successful long pass before the day's end.

On the bus ride home that night, my teammates were more than a little disappointed to hear of my cowardly turnover. The truth is, I failed to think through whether I really wanted the plan to succeed. None of us were high on stealing, but we had gotten caught up in the excitement of surreptitious planning.

Our youthful escapade was exhilarating. It was memorable.

But for me, it foretold a challenging future. Soon after graduating high school, I would attempt another spectacular catch. Only then, I wouldn't see a fenced-in parking lot. I would wake up to a newly fenced-in world.

*Mother, Deloris Meador, 1964*        *Father, Joel Francis Meador, 1968*

*David with sister Mary K.*

# CHAPTER 1

# POLICE CHASE

The police car lay mortally wounded in a desolate soybean field in Southern Illinois. Like a giant cat, the cruiser was stretched out on all fours up an embankment just beyond a ditch at the end of the road. I sat slumped in the front passenger seat, barely conscious. It was 1:30 in the morning, the early hours of Christmas Eve, 1966.

From the rear, it didn't appear that the car had much damage. The front end, however, revealed the force of the impact. The vehicle had jumped the ditch and slammed into the embankment. The front bumper, engine and frame chewed into the frozen ground. The shiny hood of the car buckled over the engine, jutting up like a mountain range. The windshield stayed intact, but was riddled with cracks, turning it into silvery spider webs against the night sky. My face was battered and swollen beyond recognition from its direct impact with the dash. Blood dripped onto the open glove compartment door.

Up to that moment, it had been the best year of my life. I was 18 years old. For the first time, I had a real job, I was making real money, and was certainly having no trouble finding places to spend it. I had nearly finished my first semester of community college, and I had plenty of friends plus a steady girlfriend. But now, lying critically injured in a crumpled city police cruiser, my world was instantly changed.

The police officer stood outside his driver-side door. "David, just hold on." Bob's words clawed and scratched across the frozen night air into my woozy head. His voice turned away from me as he took a rasping breath and looked back up the hill for the red flashing lights of an ambulance. Still gasping for air, Bob continued scanning the dark scene as he leaned against his door that had been forced open by the impact.

The officer coughed out the words, "David, I ran to a farmhouse. They let me in to call for help." Holding his broken arm tight to his body, Bob's voice trembled with pain and fear. Suddenly, my officer friend wasn't such a tough guy after all. Bob took another breath in the icy darkness and spoke again, "David, can you hear me?" He paused for a moment. "David?"

Getting no response, Bob knelt on the driver's seat and used his good arm to reach across and drape his heavy leather police jacket over my shoulders and chest. My head and upper torso had been thrown forward in the crash. Blood and mucous oozed from my battered eyes, nose, and mouth. I thought my eyes were closed, but later learned they were swollen open, eyelids turned inside out.

My head felt heavy, like a leather medicine ball in an old-fashioned gym. My heart felt the unbearable weight you feel when you know good people are going to be hurt by what you have just done. I was in the wrong place at the wrong time, and I knew this was partly my fault.

Seat belts? We had foolishly refused to wear them. This might seem incredible given today's emphasis on safety, but the Federal Government had just begun to require standardized factory installation. These were not shoulder harness restraints, but simply lap belts. Our response to this government mandate was to sit on it – the belt, that is. We all thought we were strong enough and quick enough to brace ourselves in the event of any small town collision.

In a God-given state of shock, I felt almost no pain in my face or head, but in the pit of my stomach coiled a gut-wrenching sickness. No doubt Bob felt the same. We were in an unyielding reality, both hoping to wake up and discover it was all a dream. But tonight, that wasn't going to happen.

How did I get the part of police passenger in this movie scene? Back then, I attended a nearby junior college during the day. But in the evenings, from 4:00 p.m. to midnight, I worked as second shift radio dispatcher for our town's police department. My duties:

answer the phone, dispatch an officer if needed, and maintain the station's typewritten log of police activities including tickets written and the details of an occasional arrest. I would dispatch an officer to an accident, or to a domestic dispute. Each time an officer needed to step out of his car, he would radio me to report his "10-9" – location and purpose.

My job was seldom glamorous. Summer or winter, I dragged out a long hose from the jail area in the back, washed off the sidewalk out front, and used a push broom to scrub standing water over the curb. All the while I was listening intently for an incoming call on the telephone or the radio, both turned to full volume. At the time of our car crash, I had been employed for five months and knew that my second shift responsibilities were important.

It was actually my father who got me the gig. Dad knew the chief of police. Their friendship started when my dad was just a boy. As a youngster, Dad needed spending money and guidance due to the divorce of his parents. This man, who later became the chief of police, gave my dad a continual flow of small job leads and served as the father figure he was lacking. No doubt, due to their long friendship, Dad thought his decision to get me a job working for the chief would put me in a safe environment. He also intended to occupy my night hours, which might otherwise have been spent drinking or driving around town, activities my friends and I were just discovering.

Ten minutes before midnight, Big Richard, a friend and fellow recent high school graduate, stepped into the station. He took three paces and stood at the front counter. I sat at the microphone in our little radio dispatch office dressed in khaki pants, long-sleeve shirt and cool tie, eyeing him suspiciously. It wasn't as though Richard had no business being there. After all, he held the job of dispatcher for the day shift. His shift was the busier one, the more administrative one, and the one that would eventually lead him to a successful career as the owner of a private security firm.

Richard's objective at the moment was the same as mine. "Is Detroit Bob scheduled to work tonight?" he asked. "Def-o-nitely," I crooned across the counter. Our burning desire at this late shift change was to catch Bob at the start of his work night and ride with him on his back-alley patrol route. It wasn't the route that appealed to us. And while we both admired Bob, this tough officer hired in from Detroit a year earlier, it wasn't his company either.

Richard and I waited for Bob to round the corner and park his personal vehicle. He would then take one of our two city police cars and patrol the rest of the night. The set of police wheels he was to drive this third shift was a special car, one newly acquired by the city. This was no boring police cruiser. What Richard and I were drooling over was a brand new burnt orange Dodge Polaris, a car with style and anticipated speed.

The two of us were giddy with childlike anticipation, our feelings reflecting the Christmas lights glittering on the Courthouse Square across the street. We knew our officer friend might allow one of us to cruise with him for an hour or so to begin his shift. These ride-alongs were few and far between, but since the holidays had just begun, there was no school tomorrow, which made tonight our best chance. We knew from experience that Bob wanted only one passenger and would not allow both of us to come along. He was thick-muscled, tough looking and tough talking. When Bob brought in someone for disorderly conduct, there was no doubt who was in charge. He wasn't someone you would want to cross, but he reached out to us as young guys he knew he was impressing. And we felt we impressed him too, especially with our knowledge of the town and some of its characters.

The third shift dispatcher capably took my place behind the microphone. Richard and I leaned nonchalantly against the two glass doors inside the front of the station, neither of us willing to acknowledge the race that was about to take place. As soon as we spotted Bob walking from his personal car to the police cruiser, we sprung into action, bolting out the twin glass doors, running shoulder to shoulder.

You would think a city police department would have a strict policy prohibiting civilians from riding along for the fun of it. But this was 1966, prior to the litigation fears that would follow years later. After all, this was a quiet town of 6,800 people, with little of consequence happening from evening to evening.

I, of course, won the race. Looking back, would I rather Richard had won this sprint? Would I rather have seen him in the passenger seat where his life would have changed so drastically instead of my own? Unconditionally, no. It seems to me now that what happened was meant to be.

Detroit Bob and I cruised the backsides of the downtown business district for an hour or so. Bob slowly maneuvered our warm police car through alleyways and behind buildings. Both of us shined spotlights onto back doors of familiar businesses vulnerable to nighttime break-ins. We talked about his younger years in Detroit and his stint as a member of the Military Police in Vietnam. We talked about the better life he had secured for himself and his family in our quiet little town. We exchanged ideas as peers, as adults, as friends who valued one another's opinions.

Just a few minutes past 1:00 a.m., we drove our newly-equipped cruiser toward a downtown four-way intersection. Casually, Bob and I noticed a 1962 light blue Chevrolet Impala approaching our intersection from the north. It was not a local car. Yet we both remembered seeing it on the main thoroughfare fifteen minutes earlier. This time, the driver ran the light. He swung right at the intersection and sped ahead.

"Here's a ticket," Bob said. He flipped on the dual overhead flashing lights and punched our car forward through the intersection and up the main drag, fully expecting the car ahead to pull over. Instead, the driver increased his pace. Bob and I grabbed our respective spotlights, his plastic twist handle just to his left and mine to my right. We cast our beams back and forth across his inside mirror, but still he refused to yield. Instead, he shot left onto a side street leading south out of town. We reached the same corner in seconds, turned left, and began full pursuit, lights flashing and siren wailing.

Our heartbeats accelerated with our speed. As neighborhoods blurred into countryside, the officer yelled across to me, "Do you know this road out of town?" "Yes," I shouted back assuredly – though in my mind, I was not so sure.

Bob jacked up the speed of our eight-cylinder Dodge muscle car. The dual beams of our headlights pointed skyward as we charged up a ramped railroad crossing. Our potential felon sailed ahead and just out of range for us to read his license number. Bob boomed out directives, "David, take over the microphone. Tell the station where we are and where we're headed!" I complied, confident I was assisting in the pursuit of a major criminal.

Telephone poles and houses flew by as we sped up and kicked the car to its peak acceleration. Cold wind buffeted the windshield. Revolving red lights reflected like strobes, bouncing off trees, fences and buildings in the night. Our police siren screamed for the car in front to stop. Microphone in hand, I interrupted all radio traffic as I yelled over the engine and wind noise to let the neighboring town and our own radio dispatcher know what was going on. We were caught up in the passion of the moment.

Passing a dark stand of woods, our guy cornered right onto a slightly narrower road, with Bob and me quickly following suit. Dense woods on either side of us intensified the sound of our engine and siren. Seconds later, we rocketed up a steep hill like a flare against the night sky. As we crested the hill, I again saw our guy's red taillights. To our surprise, he had already made a tight left turn onto a T-street at the bottom. But for us, racing downhill at 60 miles per hour on a gravel-strewn blacktop surface, there was no chance to turn left. No chance to turn right. Our only choice was to plow into the road-ending embankment straight ahead.

Tires screamed. Rubber burned. We were thrown into a terrifying skid – a skid that ripped us irrevocably from one life to another. The last thing I saw was Bob's heavy black shoe stomping hard on the brake. BANG! Lights out.

# CHAPTER 2

# BEGINNING OF HOPE

Bob and I plowed headlong into a stubborn soybean field that had no use for us. We found ourselves in a remote area perhaps six or seven miles out of town. Farms, woods, and open fields stood unperturbed under the night sky. A state police car and a city ambulance tried their best to find us without success. It was actually an extraordinary citizen whose actions were most helpful. Duard Duncan, a middle-aged Civil Defense volunteer, heard our chase in progress. He picked it up on his home police scanner shortly after 1:00 a.m. when he had heard me yell into the microphone to alert the nearest community. "That's right! We're coming your way, south." Duard had to wait through several seconds of silence between transmissions before he could again hear my response. "Yes, yes! 10-4! That's the same road all right. We're coming your way, fast!" That was the last transmission Mr. Duncan heard from me.

He didn't know why we lost radio contact, but he instinctively took action. Leaving the warmth of his home, he jumped into his car and drove to the countryside. He retraced our path as he had heard me describe it. But when Duard got to the side road, he followed his intuition and turned right, between the stands of woods, just as we had. He began to anticipate what might have happened as he drove up the hill that we earlier crested in full pursuit. Just over the hilltop, his headlights shone down on Bob. The officer stood at the side of our car and waved his good arm high in the air for help.

Bob and Duard supported me as best they could as we walked ten or twelve shuffling paces across flat ground to Duard's late model Plymouth. I was semi-conscious, yet aware enough to turn loose of Bob and Duard once we reached the car and its open back door. There I felt my way onto the back seat and lay down on my stomach. Duard got behind the wheel and headed toward the local hospital. As we drove up and down those country hills, the officer held his left hand on my back to keep me from rolling forward. But the changing momentum of the car pulled and tugged at my limp body each time we dipped or slowed. I eased out from under Bob's grip to the floorboard, feeling its warmth before losing consciousness altogether.

"Ace, can you hear me?" It was my dad gently trying to wake me sometime during my first day at Barnes Hospital in St. Louis. His voice entered my head through a fog, but I had no energy to respond. Dad called me "Ace" because he was so proud of the two hole-in-ones I had as a teenager. Golf. It wouldn't be the topic of choice anytime soon.

The preceding hours must have felt like a lifetime to my dad. He and Mom were awakened at 3:00 in the morning. Dad picked up the phone to hear, "Mr. Meador, I'm sorry. Your son has been in a serious car accident."

Dad drove straight to our local hospital, called Mom with the details, then followed my ambulance 70 miles west to Barnes Hospital. He told me later that Mom cried through the night, worrying about what she didn't know. As much as my mom wanted to drive along with Dad to the hospital, she had no choice but to stay at home, and later break the news to my three younger sisters and 6-year-old brother. She would never know all the details, and never see my initial injuries first-hand. This was a time of strict separation of duties between husband and wife. Her responsibility was to care for the children at home, Dad's responsibility was to shoulder the difficulties of life outside.

Dad quickly learned that my condition was critical. Yet when he returned home from St. Louis that first night, Christmas Eve, he told the family not to worry. "David's going to be fine." Mom would later characterize Dad's confident approach with a heartfelt compliment. "David, with a family of five children, Dad handled things like you knew that he would. He protected us."

Christmas afternoon, Dad drove back to Barnes to see me.

Sitting near my bed, he would occasionally stand and repeat his earlier words. "Ace, can you hear me?" Finally, I recognized his voice. As soon as he felt I could listen and understand, he told me where I was and why I was there. Instantly, the car chase replayed in my head. It was like seeing it inside a darkened theater; only the action played at high speed.

The next thing I was conscious of was a papier-mâché mask of bandages across my face. Cloth strips held down medicated dressings over my eyes, cheeks and nose. Restrained by a miniature jail of wire braces, my upper teeth swayed and tilted from the pressures of a curious tongue. A diagonal pin stuck out through each cheekbone. A rubber tip marked the top of each pin, giving me the look and feel of Frankenstein.

There was more. Behind my upper lip, a slender steel rod had been inserted vertically. It extended upward behind the inside of my front teeth to hold in place the center septum of my nose. A question kept running through my mind: *How will this spike be removed?* I found out later, gripping the arms of an outpatient surgery chair. It was twisted out manually.

Add to all of this a problem with breathing. My nostrils were densely packed with gauze, causing me to breathe by mouth. Caring nurses helped me drink and eat through a straw, repeatedly salving my lips with ointment. My situation was painful, tedious, confined, and uncomfortable – and allowed me plenty of time to think.

During the first week or so in the hospital, my thoughts kept hanging on to those wires and spikes. At first, I didn't think much about my inability to see. I really had no desire to open my eyes, even when bandages were being changed. Or maybe I just wasn't willing to face one more problem. Nurses, and occasionally my doctor, would remove the gauze, lift up my eyelids, and shine a light into my pupils. "Can you see anything?" No. "Can you this time?" No. "How about now?" No, no, no.

After two weeks, I began praying the Lord's Prayer in earnest. I prayed hundreds of repetitions. It didn't change the prognosis. But when you have nowhere to turn, you appreciate the irreplaceable sanity that comes from talking with the only one who stays with you around the clock, regardless of circumstance. My appeals to a loving God gave me strength, but my circumstances remained the same.

During my fourth week in the hospital, the surgeon stepped into my room. Dad stood at his side. It was time. They needed to deliver the news. The doctor did the talking, "David, we have done everything possible." I listened. Seconds passed. He continued. "Unfortunately, testing shows that the optic nerve behind your eyes is irreversibly crushed. I am sorry to say…" The doctor waited a few beats to be sure his words were clear. "I am sorry to say you will never see again."

How should a young person, or any person, react to such news? How should a teenager feel, or show that feeling in front of others, especially when dealing with death? Yes, death. This was not only the loss of my eyesight, but the loss of a life that used to be. A life that was no more.

I did not cry. For whatever reason, I just couldn't. Yet I *felt* plenty. My mind seemed to implode. Bodies, furniture, walls – everything flew in a single direction. My entire world collapsed. Suddenly, everyone catapulted past me toward the future, while I remained stationary, as dead in the water as you could possibly be. Junior college classes, my friends, basketball in the backyard, driving around town, my mom and dad, brother and sisters – all flew past me, all of them high in the sky and worrying about me down in the ocean below, but unable to throw me a line.

It wasn't just that I would never be able to see them again. No, it wasn't just the seeing part. It was also the devastating realization that I would never be able to keep up with anyone ever again.

In front of the surgeon and my dad, I simply could not show my feelings. There was too much spinning in my head. I couldn't talk. I couldn't move. Soon another wave rushed over me. Surely my doctor's case-closing words were God's way of telling me I was guilty. Guilty of not coming straight home from the police station at midnight. Guilty of winning the race with my friend to the patrol car. Guilty of not wearing a seat belt. Guilty of telling Detroit Bob I knew those back roads when I didn't.

My insides also churned with another painful concern. Deep

down, I needed and wanted to protect my dad. Here he was, a former Marine and father who would never want us to think he was overwhelmed. But I knew his heart was battered and broken by this accident, an event that would irrevocably change both of us. He believed this disaster was entirely preventable. It seemed that the main thought in his mind was, "Bob should never have had David in the car in the first place." He wanted to rewrite the past, the present, and a future he knew would be filled with pain.

Some in our town speculated that Bob and I had been out field-testing the acceleration of the new police car. But Bob and I had no trouble sticking to our story, because it was the truth. The pale blue Impala and its driver got away. I'm guessing he too got caught up in the passion of the moment. He sped into the December darkness, along with the explanation that might have given light to our chase, our accident, and its consequences. I heard later there was speculation that the mysterious driver was from a nearby town, but there was never proof. As for me, I didn't really care. The "who" and the "why" meant nothing to me. I was blind, and that was never going to change. That man had fled the town for good, leaving my ruined future in his wake.

The first few days home from my six-week stay in the hospital were difficult. Without any conversation or discussion, my dad showed up in my room every night at bedtime. He brought in a pallet to sleep on the floor next to my bed. He was hurting over my situation, and I was hurting over my situation and his, but we could not talk. We simply didn't have the tools or the experience. My guess was that Dad was staying close because he didn't know what to expect from me. At the very least, he wanted to be sure I had help getting to the bathroom and back to bed. A social worker at the hospital had given me a long straight white cane, nearly chest high, with a crook on the end. I kept it standing in the corner near my door but hardly ever used it, not even to find my way to the bathroom or down the stairs. It was a symbol of my drastic life change, so I initially shunned it out of spite, resistant to being forced into a new identity, content to let it rest quietly in the corner. Within a few days Dad moved out, seeing that I was stubborn enough to get around the house on my own without too much trouble.

My friends didn't know what to expect from me either. They remained loyal and solidly behind me, but there was a hesitancy and strained energy about them. Likewise having no experience or vocabulary for the situation, their reactions were a bit comical to me.

One of my buddies insisted that I could simply correct my vision with thick glasses like his. Another friend came over and talked with me as though nothing had happened. I began to wonder if he even knew! I became afraid to get up to go somewhere, even to the bathroom, for fear he would ask, "Why are you walking so slowly?" He was surely aware, but I guess not bringing up the subject was his way of coping.

A third friend brought over his electric guitar, minus the amplifier. He carried it upstairs to my room for a visit. Although he had not played the instrument since an initial handful of lessons a Christmas or two back, he insisted on entertaining me. His renditions came complete with gyrations and frenzied strumming. He sang imitations of James Brown and Elvis in alternating dynamics – loud and louder. I hopefully was his first and only audience.

As for my girlfriend, who was in her first year at an out-of-state college, our only communication was through brief and infrequent phone calls. We were both trying to deal with the changes in our lives, and it was difficult to find common ground.

As my mobility skills were next to naught, my friends knew I was isolated. They had their jobs, their continued schooling, and their occasional parties. Still, they tried to get me out of the house and back into our former wild and crazy times whenever they could.

One of those times was a winter pastime most familiar to those north of the Mason-Dixon Line. In Illinois we called it bumper skating, and this night it came out of nowhere. I had just finished one of Mom's wonderful home-cooked dinners. But beyond the kitchen, my options were not so appetizing. One was to spend the evening "watching" TV. The other was to cloister myself up in my room to study the Braille alphabet and its assortment of single-letter abbreviations: c standing for the word can, d for do, e-every, f-from, g-go, etc. These, along with hundreds of other Braille contractions, would soon occupy my writing through college and beyond.

Fortunately, the phone rang to save me from that tedium. It was one of my buddies, Jimmy Gray. He and Randy and a friend we called Jim K. wanted me to join them for a while. In a little town like ours, "join them for a while" meant driving back and forth through our downtown square looking into other moving cars for girls. My friends told me they would let me know whenever we saw some. We did, but they sure didn't seem to see us.

Jimmy turned his Volkswagen Beetle off the main drag and onto a vacant street covered with a thin layer of packed and frozen snow. Gunning the gas pedal, Jimmy slid his little car sideways. The car came to rest with a jolt, causing Jimmy to blurt out, "Hey, this looks perfect. Are you gentlemen up for some bumper skating?"

Randy guided me across slippery ice to the back of Jimmy's car. With hands gliding across the cold back bumper, Randy, Jim K., and I crouched to find our lowest center of gravity. We whooped and hollered as Jimmy let out the clutch and jerked us forward. On Jimmy's speedometer, I doubt we reached ten miles per hour. But to us, our speed felt like we were skiing across a rippling sheet of glass. Yelling and tearing up in the icy breeze, we kept our feet under us and hung on for the better part of a block. We eventually let go and skidded in a crouched position to a twirling and stumbling halt over a bumpy pavement of hardened snow. I was only one month out of the hospital, but our venture was still worth the risk. I was with my friends.

In the deepest part of my mind, I hoped this re-enactment of earlier jaunts would bring back our old times, and maybe even my sight! I was back with my friends, but there was no relief from the painful reality. It was far easier to let go of Jimmy's cold bumper that winter night than it would be to let go of my sighted world.

As weeks passed, my friends accepted my blindness, perhaps more quickly than I did. A couple of other buddies asked me to ride around town with them, and we would inevitably meet up with other friends at the Dairy Queen Brazier, the town square, and all the other usual stops. The last of my pins and wires were gone now, but I was still self-conscious about being blind, and equally concerned that my facial features were altered as well. "Gosh, David," a friend quipped, "Considering the face you had before, we think you're much improved!"

He was probably right. Regardless, my face felt different to my touch. My cheekbones were higher, and my nose shorter. Perhaps these changes were imperceptible to others, but not to me. It was unsettling. And worse, there was no mirror to verify those differences. My fears were surely magnified by a natural teenage self-consciousness. Poets say we all wear a mask, but I couldn't recall any poetic meter that would fit my situation.

I had also lost an essential that everyone takes for granted – the ability to make eye contact. It would become a permanent unease, one of the most difficult realities of blindness. Imagine the embarrassment and frustration you would feel every time you tried to tell a joke or even render a few sentences if you could not see your listener. Your friend may let his or her eyes stray elsewhere. You could find yourself questioning if your friend was still standing in front of you, let alone still listening.

The good news is that my eyes looked normal then, and still do to this day. Perhaps too much so, sometimes causing people to doubt whether my loss of sight is total. I'm sure it's initially confusing. So long as a person is speaking, I can make excellent eye contact by listening alone. But if the voice stops or moves, my imagination and eyes begin to wonder and wander.

It felt very much that way a few weeks later. On one of my rare trips out of the house, I finally got to speak with my police officer friend, Bob. He had visited me in the hospital, but it was a group visit, not a real conversation. Now we were in a much more natural setting. He had eased his patrol car into the dimly lit parking area next to a service station. My buddies happened to see him as we drove by. We pulled into a spot near Bob's car. While my friends stepped into the station, I stayed in the back seat. Bob walked over and talked with me through the open window. He was glad to see me. He asked how I was doing. He was sincere. But he said things had been pretty rough for him. Some people still thought we had been out joyriding. Others remained convinced we should not have given chase, and that as the pursuing officer he was totally at fault.

Yes, it was awkward for me, as I felt terrible for Bob. But my dad's feelings were stronger still. Dad harbored a bitter resentment of what he believed was Bob's reckless handling of our late-night chase. He told me he ran into Bob while I was still in the hospital. Bob strode Dad's way on a downtown sidewalk, but was unwilling, perhaps unable, to come face to face with my dad. Bob stepped into the street and crossed to the other side. I later heard that Bob moved back to Detroit. It seems he never again felt comfortable in our small town.

I agonized over causing others so much pain, especially my dad and Bob. I knew that I contributed to a tough situation for both. I didn't have the experience or maturity of my police officer friend, but I had the edge on formal education. I could have made a better decision. I should have had the courage to say, "Bob, I really don't know these roads. We should just back off this chase." I'm pretty sure Bob would have agreed had I said this. But for whatever the reasons of an 18-year-old boy, I didn't.

These and other thoughts bantered back and forth in my head like a family argument. The scuffle was between the past and the present. At home, my sisters and brother had struggles of their own, since their lives too were turned upside-down. They all lived with their own responsibilities and needs, yet almost all attention was directed away from them and toward me. I knew I was a heavy burden on our family. I worried whether and how this could ever change.

One evening, friends of my parents stopped by for a visit. A hand on the smooth wooden banister, I made my way down the stairs toward familiar voices. I had already passed judgment on what I considered the awkward "feel-around" clumsiness of the white cane. Certainly, I had no desire to display it here.

This seemed like the perfect opportunity to show Mom, Dad

and their friends that I was still the same – the oldest in the family and the one who could be counted on to retain his independence. At full speed, I took the last few steps as rapidly as if I could see again. Making a right-hand turn at the bottom, I used my hand to glide past the basement door and the kitchen doorframe without bumping into either. Normal as ever, I strode into the kitchen where voices greeted me with surprise and delight.

Perhaps it was simply a matter of my own ego. Maybe it was my body's automatic pilot that gave me the feeling I could speed forward solo, totally blind and without aid of the white cane. I cruised past the stove on my left and pressed forward across the open kitchen with an extended hand to welcome our guests. Just beyond the stove, I bowled over the wooden rocking chair I forgot was there. Undeterred, hand still extended, I glanced off the overturned rocker and plowed straight into a kitchen chair that had been left out from the table. It also crashed to the floor.

Slamming into reality, I shook hands with this couple, and came face to face with humiliation. In that same way, home became a constant reminder of what used to be, but was no more. By threat of further embarrassment, I simply had to learn. Even in my own home, walking could not be handled as effortlessly as before. I had to slow down to a turtle's pace. Otherwise, I was at risk of embarrassing myself, and worse yet, causing my family to be even more concerned for me.

One week later, on a Friday, I sat in my parents' living room, depressed and alone. Slouched back on the couch, I stared ahead feeling sorry for myself and tallying my losses. No longer was I attending junior college. No longer driving or running around with friends. No longer working or helping anyone. Instead, I sat "watching" TV and doing nothing. What else would you do when your friends are jumping into their cars after their last class of the day, or making plans for the weekend? You know you'll be skipping the weekend, and every weekend from this time forward. But it was at this low point that a lasting identity and passion entered my life.

Bang! A loud noise boomed from the back of the house.

The floor and the entire house shook. I startled to attention. It was my father jolting open the back door and stepping in at an unusual time, 3:00 in the afternoon. And this, a workday! I heard Dad's heavy stride pass through the kitchen and into the carpeted hallway. He flipped up the metal latch to our basement door, opened it, and pounded down the stairs past rustling coats hanging on the wall. No sooner down, he pounded back up. He was obviously focused on an urgent task. Abruptly, he entered the living room and placed before me, of all things, my golf clubs!

Instantly, the sound of clubs rattling in their sturdy upright golf bag told me what my dad had in mind. Still, I could not believe he was standing there. "David," he paused, perhaps out of the absurdity of it all, and then continued. "David, I've got an idea. I think there is a way for you to stay in the game." I had found a kind of comfort in my pitiful depressed state, and felt my dad's efforts were completely off the mark. I thought about saying, "Dad, believe it or not, I'm in *no mood* for golf!" But I've got to say, my dad wasn't the kind of man you would argue with. Once he committed to an idea, he was going to carry it out.

My clubs rattled and clanked as Dad squeezed us out the back door and onto the concrete patio. Down five steps, onto the rocky driveway, and into the car, the three of us took our usual positions. After a tense six-minute ride up Marion Street and across two sets of railroad tracks, Dad swung his car into the parking lot of our country club. Quickly he opened the trunk, handed me my golf bag and, taking my elbow guided us onto the grass of the No. 1 fairway.

Dad pulled out a club. He touched the back of my left hand with the grip as he handed it to me and said, "David, just take this and warm up a bit." I used both hands to push the club high and horizontal over my head to stretch my back and arms. I brought the club down and began taking half cuts at an imaginary ball. Soon I was taking full swings in the crisp winter air. It felt surprisingly good.

For me, my dad was Eli Whitney, Thomas Edison, and Alexander Graham Bell all combined. It was years later before I fully understood the significance of that moment. He invented a new game for me – and gave me a new lease on life.

Neither my dad nor I knew that blind golfers and their coaches had been competing in National Blind Golf Tournaments for nearly two decades already. Without any model to follow, he instinctively did what other coaches do for their blind golfers today. He bent down on one knee and placed the clubhead directly behind the ball. He held the shaft and clubface in perfect position while I got balanced and comfortable. "Okay," he said, as he backed away.

I will never forget that first shot. It was a 7-iron. The ball exploded off the clubface. My hands and ears alone told me it was hit well. The ball soared high and straight down the fairway. In an instant, I realized: A blind man can play golf, and who knows what else?

The ball pierced the slate gray sky and flew 140 yards into my distant future. My dad, a man of few words, whooped with delight. "Beautiful, beautiful!" The elation in my dad's voice said everything. And at that moment, my *entire world* opened up. For the first time since my loss of sight, I felt like my old self! And I know that my dad felt it too.

Dad had faith in me and in himself, a faith strong enough to open my mind's eye to the future. On that day in the open air of a frigid golf course, Dad gave me back my game and my life. He gave me all he could. He gave me hope.

# CHAPTER 3

# REHABILITATION

Regardless of your situation, eventually you realize that there is only so much TV you can watch. There is only so much listening to radio, so much conversation, and only so much charming one another on the phone. And if you are newly blind, you crave something different, something you now consider sacred – the ability to read the printed word. Just as the body needs nutrition, the mind needs inspiration, information, and carefully crafted paragraphs. This was something I took for granted until my option to read books, newspapers, magazines, seminar handouts, maps, charts, food labels, menus and daily mail was lost forever.

Barely two weeks home from the hospital, I began training in a valuable reading alternative – Braille. My instructor was an exemplary woman employed by the Illinois Department of Rehabilitation. She came to our home bi-weekly by Greyhound and then by taxi from her office in Belleville, 50 miles west. Miss Mumford, a quiet, educated woman in her mid-30s, was the first blind person I ever met. She was impressive – independently mobile, a college graduate, and totally blind.

Allow me to interject a clarification into this narrative. If you prefer the word "unsighted" or "sightless" or "unseeing," please reconsider. The blind people I have known over the years, many of whom today remain my close friends, prefer the word "blind" to any substitute. I cannot speak for everyone, of course, but I can offer my own feeling. Blindness is an ever-intruding difficulty, not only for the blind individual, but also for anyone who is a close friend or family member. It's an impairment that does not need to be minimized or weakened. The man, woman, or child managing without sight deserves a square-shouldered word. And that word is "blind."

Miss Mumford's priceless gift of Braille would be a lifelong tool for me, but its utility would eventually expand to vistas far more elaborate than its 19th Century French originator, Louis Braille, would ever have dreamed possible. In addition to the embossed Braille page, the system is now incorporated electronically. By means of either standard or Braille keyboards and displays, many thousands of blind people have mastered the computer for various ways of data consumption and management. At the very least, these include reading newspapers, online research, and email. In mere seconds, the computer, adapted cell phone or PDA will scan the text content and convey the written word through synthesized speech or via a single-line Braille screen. Technology at work? Yes. The computer's line of Braille is displayed by a smooth surface of Braille dots, a narrow strip of "refreshable Braille" that comes alive, sentence after sentence, summoned to fingers as rapidly as the blind reader can read a line and press the "advance" key. But for me, it was literally 30 years in advance of utilizing Braille with computers that Miss Mumford introduced me to the more mundane medium at hand.

Sitting at our dining room table, Miss Mumford slid my way a simple index card. At first touch it felt like nothing more than an orderly arrangement of cookie crumbs aligned in two columns. The Braille alphabet – 26 tiny dot combinations, each representing a letter, one just above the other – was lined up on the card's left side. More important, each Braille letter was accompanied by its "raised letter" counterpart in a separate column to its right. There they were, the building blocks of Braille, along with raised renderings of the English alphabet, available for independent study and mastery, all on a flimsy paper card. How fortunate I was to have a teacher to simplify the daunting, and make it doable. And what a difference it would make!

After three weeks of working with alphabet only (Grade One) Braille, Miss Mumford brought out an advanced teaching tool. It was a business publication, *Fortune Magazine*. *Fortune Magazine*? I had no idea a business periodical like this would be printed for the blind. It was embossed in an advanced form of Braille called

Grade Two, which used abbreviations for common words. Most of this advanced Braille was over my head. But one particular headline was readable, and raised to the surface the biggest worry of our time: Vietnam. I would not have to go. I was battling a war of my very own.

It was about this same time that I realized I had to take a giant step forward. Something big needed to happen. I wanted more comprehensive training in what I hoped and prayed would be independent living. My parents were more than willing to do whatever was necessary to get me back on my feet. Still, they had mixed emotions during those early stages. On one hand, they wanted to protect me at home in my changed life without sight. On the other, they knew it was critical to push me out of the nest and into the world. In late March, only two months after coming home from the hospital, I headed back out the door. I was excited to be moving away from home with the promise of independence. With my carefully packed luggage in the trunk of Dad's car, we drove north up Interstate 57 toward the big city of Chicago. We didn't know what to expect. Arriving at an urban institutional setting was like landing on a different planet for both of us.

"Rounding of wall corners is one of the ways we protect the newly blind." So explained the administrator of the Illinois Visually Handicapped Institute in Chicago. He gladly guided us on a mid-afternoon tour. "Rounding of corners?" Sure enough – we were rounding several. Once Dad left, I was all alone. But I soon settled in this new environment, with new people. There was no alternative. And I would quickly learn firsthand what "rounded wall corners" meant.

Imagine yourself blind, traversing solo down a long corridor in this strange building for the very first time. You would make your way with only the help of a slender white cane. Your desired destination might be the administrative offices in the opposite wing.

Swinging your cane left and right in front of you, you would tap-tap-tap down the long stretch of hallway that echoed straight ahead. You would use your cane to touch the wall to your right every four or five steps to reassure yourself you were still headed straight. Upon reaching the building's open front foyer, you would suddenly find yourself involuntarily turning loose of the wall on your right and flying solo. This is because the walls float away from you left and right in sweeping arcs, like precision Navy jet planes peeling away from formation, and leaving you in the middle to proceed on your own. This unsettling openness would offer little more than a slight change of air pressure and a very wide listening prompt, telling you that if you want the administrative offices you'd better keep flying straight. But if you veered just ever so slightly, so imperceptibly to the right or left in this ocean of air, you would find yourself dizzy with confusion. You would run into reality, feeling with your hands one of the curved walls on the other side. But which side, right or left? You would feel the sudden barrier and ask yourself, "Where the heck am I?"

I never mastered this "open expanse" challenge, but I found the rehab training environment helpful when I was finally free to walk in more conventional structures with square corners. Despite the rehabilitation institute and its top architect, the truth is substantially more straightforward. Ninety-degree corners are vastly easier to recognize and negotiate. But through my experience in Chicago, I quickly came to learn an even broader truth. Walking with only the aid of a white cane meant learning to slow down and listen, listen for every conceivable clue, instead of depending on the automatic pilot of sight.

Perhaps now you can appreciate the carefree motion you enjoy striding from one side of a building to another, and the unfettered way you stroll across a parking lot. I was sure it would never again be carefree for me.

The broad range of adult trainees residing in this rehabilitation institute added to my distress. I was thrown in with people of all ages and backgrounds. Population diversity is something we recognize today as healthy and broadening. But for an 18-year-old used to Mom's cooking and the isolation of a small town, it was quite a culture shock.

Between the classroom section and the dormitory, a student lounge provided students a place to relax and talk after classes were finished for the day. From the classroom area you would walk down a short flight of stairs, continue past the lounge, then up a short flight to the two-story wing of dorm rooms. The lounge was empty, or mostly empty, during the regular class hours each morning and afternoon.

As a newcomer, audible landmarks like this were important. This student lounge offered the idle tones of a water cooler and the steady hum of a soft drink machine. So in the daytime, I would walk past this open room tapping my white cane and listening for its vivid and reassuring sounds of emptiness. But when the rehabilitation facility's staff left us at the end of the workday to the supervision of the night watchmen, this lounge took on a completely different feel.

At night, the room filled with subdued radio music and hushed conversations, making it seem more like an after-hours hotel bar minus the alcohol. Men and women of every age paired up at tables and restaurant-type booths. This was a mixed community that was temporary in nature, but people being people, some took advantage of their close proximity. It seemed like a high school party, only the students attending were age 18 to 60.

I will never forget calling my girlfriend long distance that very first night. I was proud of myself for being able to find the phone booth on the side of the crowded lounge with less trouble than expected. The phone was often in use, clearly identifiable by coins dropping with clicks and chings. As the occupant finished, the hard plastic receiver would be slammed down. I would be standing only a few steps away, next on deck. The person's exit would never be quite complete until he or she first checked the metal scoop for a possible windfall of forgotten coins. Invariably, the sound of that familiar pop of the scoop signaled the caller's exit and, at last, my turn.

I pulled several coins out of my pocket. Miss Mumford had taught me the trick of identifying coins by touch. She taught me what now seems obvious – edges are smooth on pennies and nickels, but ridged on dimes and quarters.

Talking to my girlfriend, I spoke with uncharacteristic

declaratives. "Guess what? This place is a zoo! You will not believe the people here." I went on to describe my situation, the lounge, blind people in seemingly unfriendly cliques, and the strange environment as a whole. This would be one of the last times we would speak as boyfriend and girlfriend, as our lives were taking divergent paths. She had her own challenges in school, while I was learning to deal with the transition to life as a blind person.

"One dollar and fifteen cents, please," the operator interrupted halfway into my call. Cradling the receiver on my shoulder, I pulled out four quarters and two dimes, and fumbled in the coins. "Just keep the change," I told the operator. I took a deep breath, and continued my petty complaints.

I told my girlfriend about a man just a few paces to my left who sang Western ballads. I later found out this middle-aged man was burdened with mental problems – nothing dangerous, but serious enough to isolate him from social interaction. He sat alone on a sofa and crooned a hauntingly memorable old cowboy tune over and over again.

I now understand that this singing sojourner in no way represented the quick wit and advanced education of many blind people I have since come to know. I felt sorry for this man, but I had no experience, no perspective. And so I became especially thankful that daytime brought a completely different feel. During working hours, things were very busy and normal. Secretaries, administrators, teachers and counselors, some sighted and some unsighted, all acted upbeat and sunny. But sadly, these so-called "normal people" all went home at 5:00 in the afternoon, leaving us – the institutionalized.

As you may gather, my life-long rehabilitation has been a continuous learning curve. More than the average teenager, I struggled with the question: "Who am I, and where am I headed?" Caught between the worlds of the sighted and the blind, I soon learned important life lessons, ones that would bring me a level of comfort and acceptance of myself, blind.

For starters, I eventually got past my hang-up on curved corners, and earned the right to test my travel skills out in the city.

After eight weeks of training, from Braille to physical fitness to housekeeping chores, I was expected to pass a final examination in mobility. In this trial of city navigation, I was asked to board a bus on my own, transfer to the Chicago "L" subway, and rendezvous with my mobility instructor far away. Far away indeed – my destination was one of the busiest retail centers in the country. I was assigned to meet my instructor, Miss Kime, in the jewelry section of the downtown Marshall Fields department store.

The big day came. Walking solo, I used my cane to make my way out the rehab center door and down to the side street that ran parallel to the building. Back muscles tight with apprehension, I turned left and tapped one block up the sidewalk to busy Roosevelt Road. Happily, I got help from a fellow pedestrian who was likewise catching the eastbound Roosevelt bus. When the big city bus stopped with a screech and hiss of air, my Good Samaritan friend and I cut our small talk, waited for the doors to open, and rapidly boarded.

Once my feet were on the first step, the happy chatter of fellow riders seemed to offer a warm welcome. Just as I had been taught, I switched the cane to my left hand and let my right glide up the slanted pole toward the driver. I climbed the steps as my hand slid forward to the top and, as anticipated, located the fare box to drop my coins in. It worked perfectly, this bus-boarding technique taught to me by my mobility instructor one week earlier.

Before the driver had time to press down the accelerator and jump his bus back into traffic, I again followed my training. I reached up for the standard overhead safety rail that extended the length of the vehicle. As the bus began moving, I made my way past the front riders and eased into what I hoped was an empty seat. I suddenly felt totally out of place. Here I was, sitting blind, totally blind, on a city bus. I was thrust into an environment where I had never expected to be. But hey, I was moving forward.

Within a few minutes, the driver yelled out the stop for the State Street / Roosevelt subway. I was the first one off the bus, but the last one to make my way to the descending stairs and the cool air below. Once underground, I transferred to the noisy subway with considerable assistance from a fellow traveler. In no time, I arrived at my downtown stop, exited the train, and somehow made it back up to the warm street level just two blocks from my goal, Marshall Fields.

Once downtown, my streak of willing helpers ran out. I tapped my way more or less independently toward the morning sun. My arms, shoulders and shins glanced off parking meters, buildings and an occasional parked car jutting out over the sidewalk. And I met some poorly positioned flower boxes and pedestrians along the way. I wandered north up the sidewalk, tacking left and right like a sailboat against the wind. Finally, I bounced into yet another pedestrian who confirmed I had reached my assigned destination.

Entering Marshall Fields exhausted and windblown, I probed my way cautiously past wooden display bins and racks of clothing. Then, with a touch of guidance from a sales clerk, I reached the jewelry department in the back of the store. "Congratulations, David, you did a great job," my mobility instructor spoke from behind me. I quickly recognized her voice and turned to greet her. What I didn't know was that she had silently tailed me from the beginning. I was caught unaware, but proud indeed that my instructor had seen every step of my accomplishment.

Still, there was a downside. Reality hit me. After all, this little jaunt from bus to train to a downtown destination was an easy trek for thousands of city dwellers every day. I saw more clearly than ever the stumbling reality of my own life to come. Nothing would be easy.

At this point, I couldn't help it. My emotions reeled. I thought I would cry. But instead, I began to whine about my frustrations. "Miss Kime, I'm telling you honestly, I am really, really tired. I am tired of crashing into people. I am tired of ricocheting off parked cars and walls. I am tired of bumping into every possible thing!"

No doubt, my instructor had to don a different hat here. She needed to be more than an instructor, more than just an employee. She needed to be strong, understanding, and wise. And so she turned to me without hesitation. Putting her hands on my shoulders as though shaking some sense into me, she looked right at me and said, "David, you did really well in this mobility test. But you're tired of bumping into every conceivable thing?" She paused for emphasis. "David. Listen. Don't you know by now? You are *supposed* to bump into things."

*Did I hear this right? Wow! Maybe my expectations have been a bit unrealistic. I'm supposed to bump into things? I'm supposed to continually glance off of parking meters, newspaper stands, people, frustration and embarrassment?* At age eighteen, I converted this independent travel lesson into a liberating life philosophy. We are set free by knowing it's okay to be less than perfect. Maybe even a whole lot less than perfect!

Whether we are cringing over social gaffs, personal missteps, financial losses, or even character lapses, do not let bangs and bruises hold you back. Think about it. The next time you pick yourself up after an embarrassment or a defeat, don't be upset. Don't be discouraged. Just remember: If you are reaching out to an unseen future, you are bound to bump into things. And you know what? You're supposed to!

# CHAPTER 4

# NEGOTIATING COLLEGE

My life in Chicago rolled on. The city had become a magical place to me, an invigorating environment where growth and change could happen more rapidly than in a small town. In a place like Chicago, you don't have to be your old self any longer. You can undergo a complete makeover, and almost nobody notices. Almost nobody cares. Not so in a small town, where everyone knows everybody. In a small, close-knit community, any sudden floundering creates a noticeable splash. Chicago was a surprising breath of fresh air, with nobody noticing that I was not the same person I used to be. In so many ways, I was splashing and making waves. And in doing so, I found the freedom to accept, to change, and to become a man – a blind man.

My first two months in Chicago at the state-of-the-art Illinois Visually Handicapped Institute had served me well. The Institute gave me a much-needed introduction to life in a brand new world. Like blacksmiths, the instructors hammered on me until I began to take shape. Fortunately, I was malleable and ready for reshaping.

Then in May of 1967, only five months after losing my sight, I moved to the next level. The Institute informed me that just down Roosevelt Road stood a sister institution, an equally respected education and training facility known as the Chicago Lighthouse for the Blind. They offered a new residential college prep program. It emerged as a godsend, at a time and place that could not have been more perfect for me.

How could these two rehabilitation facilities have stepped into my life with such perfect timing, and both in the same city? Surely, it was more than a coincidence. The Illinois Visually Handicapped Institute gave me the essentials in blindness adaptation training, and now the Chicago Lighthouse offered me and other students a summer program to prepare for college. Perhaps my prayers in the hospital were being answered after all.

The Lighthouse arranged off-site dormitory housing for 25 students. All were recent high school graduates, some partially sighted and some, like me, totally blind. Each student moved in for the summer from their homes in the Chicago area, and some from even further out in the Midwest and the South. We lived together near Chicago's South Side within easy reach of Cook County Hospital, surrounded by the frequent sounds of ambulances and police sirens. Each morning we walked, in small groups or as individuals, three neighborhood blocks to the Lighthouse building. I pictured it as a distance not much farther than a long par-five from our dormitory. No one else seemed to get the comparison.

As a 19-year-old dealing with blindness for just a few months, I was a novice caught up in a challenging new world. I was doing my best to cope with the tedious pace of living by touch, Braille and white cane. These were touchstones far different from my guitar-playing friend's 1966 metallic blue Chevy Malibu Super Sport I used to covet, and even drive on occasion. Then, out of that same shade of blue came a living flashback.

Bang, bang, bang! I jolted awake from a Saturday afternoon nap. Somebody was knocking on my dormitory door. The evocative sound of the latest hit by Aretha Franklin drifted in through my open bedroom window. Surprise! Three of my old run-arounds from home had arrived, ready to party. These were mostly the same guys that got me out bumper skating in what seemed like a lifetime ago. Even though I had turned loose of the icy bumper, I was still having trouble letting go of my previous sighted life. Now it didn't matter. The guys were here and wouldn't take no for an answer!

As we drove away from my dorm that summer evening, my friends and I turned up the car radio. We talked and laughed over the blare of our favorite tunes. Feeling the spirit of the music and the sultry night air, we ended up at a South Side tavern where we bought beers without being carded. Before we knew it, we were playing an improvised game of pool.

How would I compete in billiards? The same as with bumper skating earlier in the year – I would get help from my friends. Stepping forward this time was Jim K., a guy known for his willingness to give most anything a try. His first objective: to assist me in getting the 6-ball into the side pocket. He guided me to the correct quadrant of the table. Reaching around my right side from behind, he positioned me and the pool cue, sighting down the stick to the ball. He provided the finer adjustments to our aim by assisting me from the southpaw side of the stick. There we were, both of us leaning over the table and reaching for the cue ball, mirror images of one another. Did this work? Not at all. But we were pleased with the way the bartender and his tavern patrons applauded the team try with great gusto.

Sunday afternoon, following the departure of my friends, I sat alone in my room. It was time to return to reality, to tomorrow and my immediate challenges beyond. In less than a month, at summer's end, I would be a fulltime student at Southern Illinois University, the same place where my high school teammates and I had made headlines with our impromptu play. Soon I would face a different game at that college, with a brand new set of challenges.

*Will my college roommate be cool about having a blind roommate? How will I negotiate an airport-sized campus and still get to classes on time? How will I step into a classroom late, in front of a lecturing professor, and still find a seat? How will I find girls to date?*

The Chicago Lighthouse College Prep Director was Dr. Walter Stromer, a faculty member at Cornell College in Iowa. As a visiting professor, Dr. Stromer taught our group with an intense sense of purpose. He knew this would be his only opportunity to make a lasting difference in our lives. And what a difference he made!

Dr. Stromer was the first blind professional I knew who competed successfully in the sighted world. He was an English composition instructor and central figure at Cornell. Prior to this, the only college-educated blind people I knew were employed solely in rehabilitation.

One of the most memorable lessons learned from our director

came through a unique teaching tactic. He brought in a visiting instructor from nearby Northwestern University to lecture us on the importance of study habits. Stepping back every three or four minutes to reinforce his theme, our guest lecturer would clang an old-fashioned iron dinner bell. As directed, with the sound of that bell we all jerked to a standing position and yelled, "There's no substitute for daily preparation!"

Preparation had likewise been a central lesson from Miss Mumford. As it turned out, her insistence on Braille gave me an invaluable skill when it came to taking lecture notes in class. Like most skills, however, you first have to learn to use the correct tools – no matter how primitive they may first appear.

The smallest portable Braille writing tool of that time, and still today, is the Braille slate. Without it, there is no way I could have taken notes in college and throughout the first twenty years of my career.

The Braille slate consists of two lightweight rectangular metal strips hinged on the short left side, allowing you to lift open the top metal piece like an alligator's mouth. You place a sheet of standard typing or Braille paper down on the bottom strip and close the upper strip onto the paper for writing.

Once the top metal strip is closed, you see four horizontal rows of tiny open windows. Each window gives you the opportunity to punch down any combination of one to six dots. Individual letters, and frequently entire words, are represented by clusters of dots. You punch the combinations with a small pick called a stylus. But here's the surprising part: You press the Braille in backwards. You punch from right to left on the page. The Braille embosses through the paper so the dots are raised on the other side. You then open the top strip, take the paper out, turn the sheet over and read the Braille in the traditional manner, left to right.

Believe it or not, once I began classes at SIU that September, I could quietly punch backwards an entire page of notes just about as fast as sighted students could write forward. But there was a catch. My writing was fast, but my reading was slow. In fact, I would have a hard time matching the pace of just about any sighted second grader. This was a deficit sure to catch up with me in later weeks. How would I be able to pour through my stacks of hastily punched out notes just prior to midterms or quarterly finals?

Solution? Each and every day, I assembled my notes and slowly turtled through each Braille sentence one word at a time. From memory as much as Braille, I dictated each sentence into a tape recorder. The resulting recordings were, to my ear, practically broadcast quality. And they were in my own voice, with inflection and emphasis on the important things to remember. Of course, this took nearly two hours of work each evening. Luckily for me, my roommate was always out, so my room became my own personal recording studio.

And yet, there were other challenges. How does a blind student read standard textbooks, especially with classes and assigned books changing every quarter? It was easy for sighted students to saunter into the campus bookstore at the start of each term and walk out with books in tow. Books for me were little more than oversize paperweights. I needed readers.

There was, and still is, a wonderful organization of volunteers called Educational Tape Recording for the Blind. They specialize in reading and recording textbooks cover to cover. At least one month before beginning a new quarter, I would purchase the assigned books from the bookstore and package them up for mailing. What a godsend! And yet, there were issues. Can you imagine being a volunteer reader, sitting before a studio microphone to tape an entire math volume of graphs, tables, and polynomial equations? Let me tell you, trying to listen to one wasn't much fun either.

Still, a pressure cooker persisted in my belly. Negotiating the campus, attending classes, eating in the cafeteria, reading notes and books, taking tests – everything required constant adaptation. Understandably, my deepest, perhaps most driving desire was to run. Not run away exactly, but run like the wind. Unrealistic as this may sound, I wanted the ability to fly down the steps of Old Main and zoom across campus to my next class. It's like every child's dream to fly, to soar above the trees and clouds. Suffocating under a load of tasks and seldom feeling I could breeze through anything, I at least wanted the ability to dodge around groups of conversing students, jump over an occasional puddle, and dash full stride down a maze of sidewalks winding across the campus and the town.

I suppose what I really wanted was to see. But all I could see was the truth. Running across campus just wasn't going to happen. At least, I thought, I should somehow have the ability to walk briskly, smoothly and confidently like normal students do every day. My longing was both physical and emotional. Being conspicuously blind on campus is one thing, but being conspicuous and stumbling is another.

Thankfully, someone else felt the same concern. A special person re-appeared – my dad. He would not have it any other way. Before each new college term, he came up for a day to serve as my personal route planner and campus guide. However, this quarterly work assignment generated unbelievable frustration and stress, as he taught me each route, then trailed me in practice. Unfortunately, Dad never quite got over the emotional pain of watching me struggle to make the right decision at every road or crosswalk or overhanging bush or classroom entry or exit stairs. We would work three or four hours at a stretch. Dad simply refused to go back home without being absolutely sure I was thoroughly trained and drilled. Over and over again, he walked behind me as I tried to perfectly execute every crossing or turn. But perfect was never possible. His insistence on perfection was much to his credit, but each drill left us with neck muscles stiff with tension.

Early in my sophomore year, I met a remarkable blind student on campus. Lemuel Phipps was a young black man, two years older than I. He was barely five feet two inches tall, but thick across the chest, shoulders, neck and arms – an obvious athlete. You could hear it in his confident talk and walk.

Lem had been a successful All-State wrestler in high school. He had competed as a student at the Illinois School for the Blind. However, my friend did not earn his All-State standing simply by wrestling other blind students. "Are you kidding?" I asked Lem when I first heard him say it. His prestigious high school honors had been won by wrestling sighted athletes at regular sighted high schools across the state. Lem was like Dr. Stromer – more living proof to me that a blind person could compete in a sighted world.

My new friend showed me the meaning of white cane courage both on and off campus. There was nothing of greater interest to me than this kind of self-assurance, speed and independence. He taught me first-hand a new and exciting concept: Don't be afraid to take on the campus, the town, and the world! He presented himself, holding his white cane, with the demeanor and quiet confidence of a fencing champion. Lem did not, absolutely did not, carry his white cane as a sign of compromise. You didn't see the cane, you saw the man.

Believe me, Lem knew how to wield that foil. As he attacked an unfamiliar section of town or campus, I could feel and hear his movements as I hung onto his elbow, following his lead. Sweeping the cane left and right in front of him, he kept the business end down on the sidewalk, vigilant for stairs or holes. This was classic white cane technique – only double the frames per second. At full speed, Lem took shorter but quicker, more athletic steps for balance and abrupt stops. He would hit a campus bicycle stand with the cane, give it a loud whack for good measure, and keep moving. He could stop on a dime, shift gears, and then surge ahead. Inanimate objects had no chance.

Lem was quick. Not careless or reckless, but quick. He stayed relaxed, yet willing to make mistakes. More to the point, he knew he would make mistakes. His travel strategy was safe and straightforward: Slow down just enough to correct each error in a lighthearted fashion, then keep moving.

My friend Lem graduated a year before me, and moved back to his hometown of Chicago. He worked as a counselor in the financial aid department of Malcolm X College. He is now married and has two children. One of his daughters, despite total blindness, went to the University of Illinois and became an attorney. Lem maintained his balance and momentum through 30 years of financial aid counseling. He recently retired, and retired happy. He mastered his life, his career, and the city of Chicago in the same way I saw him master Southern Illinois University. He just kept moving.

The greatest lesson learned in four years of college was a meaningful one. Do you want to take on the world? Do you want to negotiate a difficult change of direction? Just take that first step, and keep on moving. And trust that God will provide a variety of inspiring partners along the way.

# CHAPTER 5

# MARRIAGE

I tell people I am one of the few men who actually advertised for his wife. Online dating is commonplace today, but in 1968 a man needed to be much more indirect. My own approach was so indirect that it must have been deeply hidden in my subconscious mind. It was much later that my conscious mind identified it for what it really was – a personal ad that worked.

Early in my sophomore year of college, I posted a notice in the lobby of Saluki Arms. This was the nearest women's dormitory to my own men's dorm, just two blocks away. "Blind student needs reader to help with library research and typing of term papers. $1.25 per hour."

Why the need for a regular reader? Textbooks were available on tape, but classroom handouts and library materials were not. And just as critical, there were out-of-class assignments that would require vision and skill. One of the most common was organizing and typing term papers.

"Would you please make up your mind?" Connie asked again, exhausted, as she waited with her fingers poised on the typewriter keys in the lobby of her dormitory. She couldn't help but express her impatience. I was not yet finished after two hours of fumbling through several cassette tapes, searching and dictating different bits and pieces for her to type. My term paper was due the next day. It was 10:45 in the evening, and men visiting the women's dormitory had to be out of the building by 11:00. How could we possibly finish? We did so by lugging my tape recorder and Royal portable typewriter out onto the concrete steps under the lights, where the bugs kept us company, and we worked into the wee hours of the morning.

Connie was just that way. When it came to getting things done, she was all business. That year, I enrolled in Marketing, my first business course. Nothing but lectures and class discussions filled the first few weeks. Finally, a term paper was assigned, requiring research of trade periodicals available only at the University library.

I called Connie to ask if she would be available to help me with this. The very next evening after dinner, I tapped my way down the street from my dorm to hers. Once in the library and with periodicals in hand, we sat down in a large room with a smattering of students, all with heads down, absorbed in study.

Considering myself a golfer, and having no other suitable interests to draw upon, I had chosen to write a report on the quality and marketing of golf balls manufactured by Titleist. We could not check out any of the trade periodicals, so we were forced to stay in the designated library reading room. Connie spotted a table right away in an area that was somewhat distant from the other students. Still, she kept her reading voice low out of respect for the students sitting nearby. They poured over their own reading with only the sounds of an occasional page turn or repressed cough.

As she read page after page about the Titleist Company's high standards of quality, their product attributes, uniformity, feel, inner bindings, flight, bounce and market appeal, she constantly spoke of balls, balls and more balls. Connie was 19 and I was 20, and by this time we already liked one another very much. She knew my tendency to give her a funny look whenever anything halfway sexual might be implied by the spoken word. Understandably, she could not look my way, as I was already using my sincerest facial expressions and an occasional low tone to express a mockingly exaggerated interest. Each sentence became a monumental reading task. The word kept popping up. Our eyes teared. Chokes of laughter kept exploding within. We shook with stifled laughter; both of us trying our best not to disturb the other students, but at the same time knowing the subject was off limits for discussion. After all, I was simply doing research, and fulfilling my scholarly responsibilities.

Connie was not only smart, slim, attractive, and responsible, she was also fun. And it was then I began to feel, at least subconsciously, that I was in love with this kindred spirit, this like personality, who yet was so beautifully different. My conscious mind, however, refused to see and feel the truth until an episode occurred, a situation that was not nearly so happy.

My father was driving me our familiar 75 miles back to Carbondale after a weekend stay at home. I leaned against the passenger door and made small talk about Connie, about my roommate, about an upcoming paper. My dad and I had already made this trip so many times. We had driven over half the distance to Carbondale when I realized I had forgotten to bring along an irreplaceable essential: my white cane. "David, don't you have a spare in your dorm room?" Why I did not have two or three extras propped up in a corner of my dormitory closet, I do not know. I explained that I did not, and so Dad turned the car around immediately, and made the trek back home. Dad didn't say anything, just drove 40 miles back home, and then another 75 miles to Carbondale in silence.

Dad's mind was most definitely still troubled, stuck on the past, unable to let go of the fact that his son was blind and blindness was not going away. Whenever we were together, he almost always seemed sad, absorbed in thoughts that must have been partly about him, but mostly about me. Yet these thoughts lay unspoken between us.

We pulled into my dormitory parking lot around 10:00 at night. Together we heaved my luggage and clothing on hangers up the dorm stairwell and into my room. My roommate was out, as usual. It must have looked a bit lonely to my dad's eyes, so he took extra care to help me unpack and get everything put away. I was tired. He was tired. Dad guided me to my closet. As he directed my hand across the tops of hangers with matched sets of clothing that he had rearranged differently from my own placement minutes earlier, I broke.

I grasped the two hanger sets of clothing he was showing me and viciously threw them to the floor. I didn't have the words to express my frustration. Dad was the constant caregiver, and I the constant recipient of his endless list of rearrangements and straightenings. Just by existing, by surviving my automobile accident and rehabilitation and now continuing to college, I had once again placed my dad in this terrible position of having to deal with the reality that seemed so painful for him to revisit. It was a reality so foreign to his own physicality – a quick, athletic and forceful approach to life.

My dad left, without receiving much of an apology on my part. I was upset in a way that was more like my dad than not. I too was tired of this unchanging circumstance, and I took it out on him. His insistence on trying to do things right resulted in an angry finish to our trip.

Late that night, I needed to speak with someone who would understand. It was past the women's dormitory's normal calling deadline. Connie was surprised to hear my voice. I had never before confided in her my deepest feelings, and, in this instance, my regrets. I picked up the phone and called her because, well, because there was simply no one else I would rather speak to at that moment. There was no one else who would listen or care. Somehow, I knew that she would. And I knew that I would – I would care for her, her listening, her response, her judgment and feelings. She couldn't say much, except that she understood what happened and how I felt. The paramount thing is she was there, and she listened. Our friendship now shared personal confidences and a new level of trust.

As time went on, Connie and I would spend many hours at the Lutheran Center, which was only a couple of blocks from her dorm. I would load myself down with books, Perkins Braille writer, tape recorder, typewriter, and assignment sheets and head down the street. She would join me in the short walk the rest of the way. The Lutheran Center provided private study rooms (with glass windows) in the basement. We used these rooms to read and talk during reading breaks. It was there that I first kissed Connie. And wow, what a kiss! Our first kiss served well as a replacement for chapter three in my three-chapter assignment. From then on, the more we tried to read, the more difficult it was to read. We shared many other kisses – sitting on the edge of the fountain in front of Old Main, along the paths through the woods between classroom buildings, and standing between the glass doors of Connie's dorm just before the manager kicked out all the males and locked the dormitory for the night.

That's the way it started in the mid-point of our sophomore year. Though we both kept up our grades and had plenty of classroom and study time apart, we were increasingly together. In the lobby of Connie's dorm, we watched John Denver and Johnny Cash on TV. The Golden Bear Pancake House served as our regular date for Sunday dinner. Once in a while, we would take a taxi to our local Village Inn Pizza, where often they would have live music and sing-along lyrics projected on a screen. One night we even camped out on blankets under the stars. We were in a grassy area on campus not far from our dorms. This was the spring of our junior year, an academic term cut short because of massive student unrest all over the country in protest of the Vietnam War and the tragic killings of Kent State students by the National Guard. Our historic and oldest university structure, Old Main, would be burned to the ground by student radicals and outside agitators within sight of Connie's dorm just a night or two after our campout.

In the fall of our senior year, Connie invited me to visit her family in a small rural town about an hour away. I saw right off the bat that Connie came from a strong family. Her father and mother were self-sustaining people who drew their life and sustenance from their 80-acre farm. In that first visit, I could see the daily demands of farming and raising a large family required all the strength and time that any two hard-working parents could muster. Their considerable skills had earlier been augmented by the contributions of ten children. Unfortunately, most of Connie's brothers and sisters had moved out of the house by the time she was seven. Connie and her younger sister were the only two left. Isolated on the farm, Connie learned by stark necessity the importance of self-reliance.

Connie went on to graduate with a double major in Elementary and Special Education. This doubling up required two full terms of student teaching in separate elementary school systems elsewhere in Southern Illinois. In each case, she was responsible for daily lesson plans, student evaluations, and classroom teaching. The demands were rigorous. During the winter of her second term of student teaching, my future wife developed a health problem.

The first I heard of her hospitalization came by way of a mid-morning telephone call. Connie was seriously ill and dehydrated from the flu. She sounded pitiful. The next afternoon she was just as sick, but when I walked into her hospital room she certainly sounded better in one regard. I arranged my visit as a total surprise. She could not believe that I took a Trailways bus from Carbondale to her student teaching location. Her voice sparkled with delight. In those first few seconds as I walked into her hospital room and heard her weakened but happy voice, it confirmed and clarified something inside of me. It was that feeling we hope and search for our entire lives. It was love I was hearing, and love I was feeling. This woman was the one, that special one whose voice and touch asked me to stay. And with this young lady, I was sure I wanted to. Our new love helped nurse Connie back to health, and we were soon ready to take our relationship to the next level.

Connie's father had no problem accommodating our need for transportation on the Saturday after Thanksgiving. A lifetime of farming made him an early riser. In overalls and in pre-dawn darkness, he drove us in his pickup to their local train depot. He didn't know that we were on our way to pick out wedding rings. All anyone knew for sure was that we were off to spend an early Christmas shopping day in St. Louis some 90 miles to the west. From the little parking area near the track, Connie's father flashed his headlights. The train rounded a slight bend, shone its bright beam of light against the darkness, and eased in to the depot.

My college sweetheart and I sat snuggling in the center car, feeling the gentle sway of the Central and Eastern Illinois railroad as we talked about our future. We were giddy with excitement. Our train pulled into St. Louis and its historic Union Station at 8:00 a.m. We bounded down the metal steps at the rear of the car and began walking to the first retail store. It was Jaccard's Jewelers, one of the city's best. We strode along the sidewalk together, my left hand holding my cane, and my right pressing Connie's sleek wool coat at the small of her back. Our attachment foreshadowed the many years of closeness we would later come to know.

The storefront glittered its early Christmas welcome. As we negotiated our way between glass counters, I noticed one of Connie's lifetime characteristics. She would spot her preference within minutes, sometimes seconds. It came as no surprise when she immediately eyed what seemed an ideal choice. Inside a glass case, a perfect set of rings within our price range reached out to us like waiting friends. Still, we spent almost an hour in Jaccard's looking at other possibilities. It appeared nothing in the store could compare. So with our initial selections in mind, we scrambled out to hunt elsewhere.

Four hours later, we completed our search through several other stores. We strode back out on the street with one conclusion. Our favorites waited for us back at Jaccard's. Of course, these were the rings Connie had discovered within the first few minutes of our arrival, but by the time we finished the paperwork, we had precious little time to catch our train. We completed and signed all of the credit forms in a flurry, and flew back out the revolving doors.

Connie's running speed and endurance en route to the train amazed me. She pulled me along at a pace that made me question whether I was still the athlete I thought I was. My lungs hissed like air brakes on an overloaded eighteen-wheeler. Connie sounded just as winded, but here's the difference: Her determination was bigger than any problems life might throw her way. We ran several city blocks in record-breaking time, and it's a good thing we did, because the train started to depart the station within a handful of seconds after we hopped up onto the metal stairway. We advanced our union in the style I would later see over and over again. We got things done to her standard – perfection.

As for asking for Connie's hand in marriage, I'm afraid I never quite orchestrated the perfect down-on-one-knee proposal that Connie so thoroughly deserved. My failure to plan remains to this day one of those goofs I wish I had handled better. But my intentions were good. I arranged for Connie to be with me at my parents' home on Christmas Eve. That night, I finally found a quiet moment to talk with my mom and dad, and let them know of my impending engagement. My timing was all very last

*Connie and David's wedding at Mt. Olivet Church, McLeansboro, IL, 1971*

minute. My proposal of marriage was delivered awkwardly in the parking lot of our church as we trailed distantly behind my family on our way to Midnight Mass. I slowed our steps to an amble. Finally, I slowed us to a stop. At midnight, we stood on

Helen Burrus Photography

*25th Wedding Anniversary*

asphalt in a darkness filled with softly falling snow.

"Connie," I said as I slipped the ring onto her finger, "please marry me?" Connie's hands holding mine so very tightly told me everything. She hesitated, and then made her answer clear and direct. Teary-eyed and glowing with happiness, she simply said, "Yes."

Connie planned our June wedding with class and precision. She had grown up attending a General Baptist congregation a couple of miles from the family farm. In my own small town, I had attended our Catholic church. To accommodate both families and both church traditions, we were married by duel celebrants. Connie's minister, Brother Raymond, and the local priest, Father Joe, linked theologies to assure this would be a wedding that would take.

I don't want to brag, but our wedding was one hot union! June in Southern Illinois brought near triple-digit temperatures. Friends and relatives eagerly stepped into the shade and peace of the little country church. Just the day before, Connie and her closest friend decorated the interior with flowers, ribbons and greenery. And the day prior, Connie had finished sewing the elegant satin and lace wedding gown of her own design. As she and her father walked down the aisle, she looked beautiful in every possible way.

At the end of the ceremony, Brother Raymond offered the traditional matrimonial invitation, "David, you may kiss the bride." Caught up in the moment as I was, I did not hesitate. The fact is I kissed Connie longer than expected. Much longer. One of my high school buddies broke through the quiet whir of electric fans with a boisterous "Amen!" Our newly bonded assembly burst into laughter and applause. We recognized our marriage was not only blessed by family and friends, but it was also blessed by God. His blessing would be needed in many events yet to come.

# CHAPTER 6

# FIRST JOB

In the spring of 1999, I was privileged to represent the United States Blind Golf Association in an international tournament in Japan. This tournament included golfers who were either visually impaired or totally blind. We were set to play the course at the popular Southern Cross Resort in Shizuoka, Japan, in the high elevations that drop steeply to the sea just south of Tokyo.

With our coaches near us, we stood patiently between practice range and clubhouse, 48 competitors from various countries around the world. Speeches blared through outdoor amplifiers welcoming blind golfers and coaches from Australia, England, Ireland, Japan, Scotland, Canada, and the United States. We were all proud to be there, and grateful to our hosts. We stood at attention, yet most of us were preoccupied with thoughts of our golf swings.

On the third hole on this sunny windblown morning, my coach and I struggled with our round. I had pulled my second shot to the left. I knew we were close enough to the green that we should be able to reach it with our next shot. The question: Which club to use?

Driving the golf cart, setting up every shot, and handling all the judgment calls that were required to coach me in this competition was Connie's 15-year-old nephew, Evan. Evan was an intelligent and most willing young man, but not yet very experienced in golf. At that moment, I could hear young Evan walking left and right. After two minutes of silence, he finally let me in on the bigger picture. "David, it's a tree." "Really?" I asked, keeping my emotions in check. "Evan, what do you think our distance is?" I waited a few seconds and queried again. "How far to the tree and then on to the green?" But his only answer was an incoherent mumble.

Standing in only moderately thick rough, and believing the ball could be struck cleanly from here, I spoke up once more. "Evan, should we try to go under?" "Yes, well, maybe. I think so, but I'm not sure," he responded with a worried break in his voice. I asked, "How tall is the tree? Could we maybe go up and over it?"

This went on until we were interrupted by a man running our way with short quick steps, loudly chattering instructions in his native tongue. It was our twosome's Japanese scorekeeper, Mr. Yamamoto. Though Evan and I knew not a single phrase of Japanese, we understood him perfectly. The rapid-fire voice said it all. He was upset that we were holding up all the golfers behind us. Knowing very little English, he reached into his repertoire of a few American utterances. Rendering his best CBS Ken Venturi impersonation, he came through with a terrific three-word summation, "Meedow," he said gruffly, "you stymie."

My memorable situation on that Japanese golf course in 1999 perfectly captured the feeling of an earlier time. As a 22-year-old, just engaged to be married, I sat at my desk in the dormitory at Southern Illinois University. I worried about my ability to find a job at all, and especially one that I could do well. The jobless rate that year, 1971, had risen to an alarming 6%. The unemployment rate among blind people was even more alarming: 85%. Why such a difference? Being blind would indeed have to be considered a problem – as judged by employers, the preponderance of whom are sighted. I could imagine thousands of them standing like a forest of trees between me and that coveted target – the American green!

Match my undeniable fear with an equally intense need to succeed, and you have the classic behavioral dilemma: "Fight or flight." Whether I would respond to my fear of failure by running away or staying and fighting depended entirely on the strength of my emotional need – my desire to get that first job.

That desire was planted early. Even as a young boy, I could see it was good to be needed by people. People relied on my dad so much that they would plead with my mom. "Please ask your husband to come out right away!" They were calling about the essential needs of farm life: cooking, refrigeration, heating, and running farm equipment. My dad supplied the fuel they needed to do those things, namely bottled gas.

At age 7, my bedtime approached too rapidly for a boy who was anything but sleepy. Outside in the dark, the temperature dipped down to the teens. One night, my dad got a call to deliver two tanks of bottled gas to a family living on a farm several miles out of town. I begged him to take me along. Dad eventually relented, and let his elbow-high son ride shotgun in the truck. I could see that my dad was really valuable, even essential, to his customers.

We were going to deliver two round-shouldered cylinders about the size of Kentucky Derby jockeys. They rode safely with us all the way. Dad rolled out the cold, clanky bottles, hooked them up to the farmhouse, and jumped back into the truck's

*Father and son*

toasty cab with me. As we pulled into our driveway and walked across the crunchy frozen yard into our warm house, surely Dad was happy. Surely, because I was.

I knew the secret to being an adult – helping people. That's the sure way to love what you do. This is the thought that was hooked up to my impressionable mind that winter night so long ago. I wanted to be needed like my dad. So years later, as my college experience neared its end, and with this motive long simmering under the surface, I forced myself to move forward.

I started by securing every interview I could. Connie and I paged through the campus calendar to look for any major employers from Chicago and nearby St. Louis who were scheduled for on-campus recruiting. I knew I wanted to live and work in a metropolitan center, where I would have access to public transportation to and from work. Besides, I had already proven that I could handle a big city, and knew I would get energy from being somewhere different from most of my old schoolmates. There was no way I wanted to go back to my old friends where I would be under the pressure of trying to live two identities – the old me and the new.

I interviewed with every visiting company possible, and I got very good at winning people over. One of my best campus interviews was with a district sales manager from Northwestern Mutual Life, Mr. Luther Haas. Mr. Haas was a man in his early 50s, and he came to believe in me. He truly loved the life insurance business, and I am convinced he wanted the best for me as a new college grad. But I was young and afraid to take on the risk of being compensated by sales commissions alone. So with this as my first exposure to Northwestern Mutual, however gratifying and uplifting it was, I turned him down.

Connie and I continued our job search for me during the late winter and early spring before our graduation and wedding. She edited and typed my resume and cover letters. We worked hard on these, and worked until we reached perfection.

Fortunately, we generated enough interest to get lots of responses. Unfortunately, every one was a form letter of rejection.

We decided the way to prove my aptitude and drive would be to send a personalized follow-up letter for every impersonal letter of rejection. This letter was simple, just an attempt to distinguish ourselves with an effort to say thanks, and to ask them to keep me in mind should circumstances change.

One of these job prospects kicked a second letter back to us immediately. It was from the personnel director at Bankers Life and Casualty Insurance Company in Chicago. "Dear Mr. Meador, call me. We want to arrange an interview." Hurray! That's all the letter said, but a sweeter piece of news Connie and I had never heard. *Fantastic – show us to the train station. We are off again to shop for a diamond!*

Ironically, at that same time, we received an equally crisp communication from the Illinois Central Railroad in Chicago. Their letter was in response to my resume and it said they were considering me as a viable candidate for railroad freight sales. And there was more. They would additionally provide rail transportation for Connie and me to our interview site, the "City of Broad Shoulders." We arranged my interview with Bankers Life for that same day.

The first interview was with the railroad. This experience turned out to be both an ego boost and bust. My meeting with Illinois Central took place over lunch at the prestigious Railroad Club, located just off Michigan Avenue. The railroad sent two sales executives, both dressed in suits, both approaching middle age, and impressive indeed. Another class act – their secretary asked Connie to join her at a different restaurant, an eatery of equal distinction.

The location of my interview was posh. But thankfully, I was dressed properly and apparently I made a good impression. The man closest to me spoke up right away. "Just take my arm. We'll follow Antonio. He has a table waiting for us." These men took me in tow and followed the waiter to our table. The room felt exclusive, much more so than any I had been in before. It was filled with lively stories being told confidently at tables all around. I began to feel like I was *somebody*.

Five minutes after sitting down, I started to relay a story I thought these men would enjoy. As often happens, just at the point of my punch line, our waiter came to our table and interrupted. In a stiff, haughty voice, he intoned, "Gentlemen. Please. Your order?"

Our waiter returned a few minutes later, skillfully placing our entrees in front of each person. We went on with our business meeting. As I had just forked into my mouth a large bite of filet of sole, one of my companions asked, "David, how do you feel you might best help our sales organization?"

My taste buds screamed from behind stressed lips. It was not fish! It was a quarter cut of lemon, rind and all, stabbing its bitterness into my tongue and sinuses. As both men looked on, I felt like I had been hit with an uppercut from Joe Frazier. How might I help their sales organization? Though my eyes watered and my face was turning yellow, I kept my composure and swallowed. I told them that I thought I could "handle most any contingency."

Later that afternoon I approached Bankers Life & Casualty, my second job possibility. Connie and I were escorted by a friendly secretary back to the private office of Mr. Jim Gawne, the personnel director. As we talked casually and in a relaxed manner, I began to realize Mr. Gawne was simply helping us get comfortable for the real interview to come.

At the four-minute mark in our conversation, Mr. Gawne picked up the phone, called his secretary sitting at her desk just twelve feet away, and told her to call upstairs. The man being called was Mr. Maguire – this was Mr. Gawne's boss, the person who liked our follow-up letter and authorized this interview. Mr. Gerald Maguire, executive vice president, was tall and spoke with a soft, Kentucky accent.

Mr. Maguire favored Connie right away. He was a ladies man, and it showed. Perhaps it was mostly because of Connie that our interview was going so well. Mr. Maguire gave us his decision immediately. He wanted me to start as a personnel interviewer one week after our June wedding. I would interview and evaluate people for insurance company jobs – from actuary to computer programmer to file clerk. Beginning salary was $650 a month. I got the job. Pure happiness!

That very afternoon, the lead Illinois Central salesman called me while we were still at Bankers Life. I had told them I would be having an interview there as well that day. When I returned his call from one of the personnel department side offices, he said they too wanted to make an offer. This was a delight and a "tasteful" affirmation of my greatest dream.

I nearly cried over my dilemma. Here I was with two great offers, one from Bankers Life and another from the well-known Illinois Central Railroad. But the truth was, Bankers Life felt like the best fit for me.

You would think I would be ecstatic. I was one month away from walking down the aisle with this beautiful young lady at my side. I had secured the job that Connie and I had worked so hard together to put me in position to win. But I was scared. I knew I would be in the spotlight, and both Connie and Bankers Life would rightfully be expecting a lot.

At first glance you might not see the pressure of reality closing in on me. My dream of performing once again in the sighted world would involve not just one job, but two. The first was the job itself, employment interviewing. The second enormous occupation would be the job of continuing to live blind, now with a wife to think about as well. I had somehow formed in the recesses of my mind the hope that graduation from a university also meant graduation from blindness. My subconscious kept whispering to me, "David, you've completed four years of college. Now, surely, you deserve your sight back!" But it wasn't going to happen.

And so again, my concerns and questions became all-consuming. *Will there be enough help at the office? Will I be able to let Connie concentrate on her new job, and not so much on mine? How will I get help reading application forms?* Surprisingly, the task of deciphering application forms was solved by my fellow workers. You might say it was "spontaneous consensus." My fellow interviewers and office staff rose to the occasion without

*David with parents at graduation from Southern Illinois University, 1971*

my asking. They stepped forward as needed to give an on-the-run summary of every application I lifted out of the box. Without making a big deal, someone would always stop and look over each completed form to tell me the salient details.

This amounted to a radical change in thinking and in routine for them, a generosity I rewarded in the only way I knew how. I worked hard and spread myself around so that no one person would feel put upon. But there was another more lasting effect on my co-workers. No one ever complained about feeling disadvantaged.

"Miss Carey. If you will please follow me back this way?" These are the words I would offer to my next applicant. Time after time, I would walk to the reception area and bring applicants back to my office in this manner. Recalling this routine, and how each appointment needed to be relatively quick and the resulting paperwork properly processed, I here disclose a decision I made early, which you may feel beyond the normal bounds of reason. In this, my first job, I "faked" being sighted. In a way, time constraints required it. We were a busy operation, five interviewers on the day shift, and two at night. Twenty-five interviews a day for each of us would not be unusual. Bankers Life was large and growing, and was constantly posting job openings because of new positions and turnover.

But back to "faking sight," and why, there just wasn't time to explain what needed explaining. My job was to get applicants to tell their story, not to tell mine. And so, faking sight suited me

*First day on the job at Bankers Life*

just fine for those few minutes with each applicant. And I'm sure I did not fake it very well, which must have created many puzzled expressions on people's faces as first I had to walk the distance, greet job applicants in the reception room, and then ask them to follow me back down a straight hallway with cubicles on either side.

Holding in my right hand the application form for Miss Carey, having just had the highlights read to me by a fellow interviewer, off toward the reception room I would walk, all the time keeping my left arm down, wrist extended outward with hand gliding across the exterior sides of cubicles lining the hallway. You might say this wall of 40 feet or so on my left served as my guide. So familiar was I with this wall, its connection seams, its openings to cubicles and the secretarial pool on my right, then another cubical on my left, that I felt alive, athletic really, fast moving, and – dare I say it – sighted!

Knowing I was expected to carry my weight in sheer volume of applicants handled, I set sort of an internal "cruise control" at what felt like 80 miles per hour. As I approached the reception area, a high-strung mid-level manager in our department, Fred, bolted out of my boss's office, turned right, and, smack! Our foreheads collided exactly like two bowling balls thrust at one another in mid air, pounding at center forehead level, snapping both necks backwards. I could not assess the extent of Fred's injury, I only knew that he was quiet, and my boss was tending to his head and asking someone to run for a wet paper towel. I stood there apologizing profusely, feeling terrible. This was not the way to win friends nor influence people. And of course, my own head, being very hard, survived this crash without any sign of trauma. Still, my head rung like a bell for a few seconds, and, not being able to see the situation, I could only stand there unheeded, apologizing in the sincerest of terms.

Standing just a step or two from the reception area, I quietly moved in that direction and announced the name of my next applicant. As was my routine, I greeted the young woman, Miss Carey, with a smile and an apology for her long wait on this busy day. Hurriedly asking that she follow me back, I carefully stayed to the left, giving Fred and his impromptu nurses plenty of room and respect.

To my surprise, the interview went reasonably well. At its finish, I thanked the young woman and explained that we could not promise anything, but we'd get back to her if her particular department of interest – claims adjusting or business correspondence – were to want a second interview. With my applicant dismissed, I could not help but sit down and reflect on the collision I had just caused, and Fred's understandable refusal to speak at all upon my profuse apology. But eventually I had to restrict my reflections in order to limit the pain, so I turned to finish the paperwork associated with this last young woman.

I wanted to write it up correctly, with a special recommendation for this impressive recent college grad. She seemed especially suited to the job she was applying for, claims adjustor trainee, demonstrating most vividly to me her ability to remain impartial, staying with the facts rather than the emotion of the situation. I thus turned to write up my notes on the designated blank spaces on her application form.

For this task, Connie had created for me an ingenious device. Upon hearing of my need to notate applications, my wonderful wife got down to business. She first cut a clipboard-sized plywood rectangle. Then, using ten small nails, she hammered them through the plywood so that an eighth of an inch of the tip protruded through the face. After each interview, I would press the application form, right-side up, onto the board. The points of the nails would punch through the paper, thus marking the blank spaces where I could type my notes. At the typewriter, I was now able to roll in the paper, feel for the perforations, and by use of pre-set tabs, type my notes and recommendations. And because of this innovation, my notes were more profuse and, aside from occasional spelling errors, more readable than any other in the office.

As for poor Fred, however, I knew that he and I would never speak about our near-concussive crash. It was too painful for both of us. Even prior to this run-in, Fred had never exactly been welcoming to me. Though he never said this to me directly, I suspect Fred did not approve of his company's decision to hire a blind man. Many people at the time, and some even to this day, are wary of such decisions; they feel companies should not be wasting time bending over backwards to accommodate blind newcomers.

Needless to say, I think such sentiments are largely ill-informed and, ultimately, short-sighted. Whatever Fred's reasoning, he never spoke to me.

# CHAPTER 7

# FIRST CANCER

The truth is alarming. You are likely to encounter cancer sometime in your adult life. According to the American Cancer Society at the time of this printing, an estimated 38% of females in America will be diagnosed with cancer during their lifetimes. For males, the probability is even higher at 44%. Thus, between one-third and almost one-half of all Americans will someday contract cancer.

Physicians tell us that our circulatory system transports through our bodies, every minute of every day, cells that mutate into pre-cancerous forms. The immune system is our number one line of defense against these mutations, a defense that works flawlessly in almost every case. Yet when we think of our bodies being vigilant every minute of every day for a lifetime, we realize it takes only a single lapse to bring on a potentially fatal struggle.

For me, it was the summer of 1972, the beginning of our second year of marriage. The possibility of cancer presented itself as a lump under my skin about the size of a small grape – barely noticeable by sight. I felt it one Wednesday morning while shaving. It rose to my touch as I ran my fingers down the left side of my neck. It was uniform and solid, but presented no pain. That's the way it seems to be with cancer. It rarely lets pain serve as an early warning.

Connie took one look and insisted we have it examined immediately. The doctor felt my neck, took an X-ray, and right away said I needed to have a biopsy. Like any good salesman, he closed the deal. Without inviting discussion, the doctor called Chicago's Bethesda Hospital to book me a room for Monday morning. I went into surgery with little apprehension. After all, I had always been healthy. I didn't smoke. I jumped rope every other day, and remained in reasonably good shape.

It was sometime in the afternoon when I woke up from surgery. Connie's voice was easy to recognize, and came from a short distance outside my door. She was talking with my surgeon. Their hushed voices started to concern me, because up to that point I had never considered that anything serious could come from this biopsy.

Connie came in and walked carefully to my bedside. "David, how do you feel?" "All right, I think. What did the doctor say?" My worried wife hesitated just as my plastic surgeon had at Barnes Hospital six years earlier. She steadied herself and said, "David, the doctor says you have cancer. It's something they call Hodgkin's Disease."

What reaction should I have shown? At 24, my reaction truthfully was blank. I'm not saying my brain was flatlining altogether, but close. Had I gotten the news today, I would have known that my father was taken by lung cancer at age 57, and my oldest sister, just three years younger than I, died of cancer at age 53. But at age 24, I had none of that experience or knowledge.

I also failed to anticipate the struggle Connie was about to endure. She had been told only that my disease was a form of cancer and its name. So she took a bus home that evening aware of only one fact. Her husband of just one year had something called Hodgkin's Disease.

When she got home to our little basement apartment, she quickly pulled out her dictionary and looked up the word. She read that Hodgkin's is a cancer of the lymph glands, most frequently striking young people. The definition gave little details beyond that, but wrapped up with devastating impact by noting that this form of cancer is usually fatal.

"How could this be?" she undoubtedly asked of God as she went to bed that night. "How could everything we have planned and hoped for suddenly end? How can I prepare David for this? Should we go elsewhere for a second or third opinion? Dear God, please help us."

Just as abruptly, the very next morning Connie would

discover that the prognosis was miraculously different. Soon after speaking with the surgeon, she walked over to me with tears of relief. "David, honey, I love you!" she said, giving me a warm hug as she leaned carefully over me. "We are so very blessed! David, the doctor tells me your biopsy shows your cancer is Stage One, the earliest possible stage of onset."

Connie continued but with a tremor in her voice. I took her hand in mine, without fully comprehending the emotional roller coaster she had experienced in the last 18 hours. "David, listen. You have got to take radiation and chemotherapy treatments. The doctor says that if you do, you will have a 90% chance of a permanent cure after ten years of no recurrence."

I had to slow down and think before I asked, "A 90% chance if I make it ten years? After radiation? After chemotherapy?" I blurted out these questions, half understanding and half not.

All she could do was squeeze my hand and share with me her great relief. "We just have to get through these treatments, that's all." I suddenly came up with a hastily conceived response. "Okay," I said. "Can we get these done this month?" "No, I doubt it," she said. Little did we know, it would be four years before we were finished.

The first step would be abdominal surgery. The surgeon explained that exploratory surgery was needed to check out whether my cancer had spread to the lymph glands running throughout my gut. As a precaution, they would also remove my spleen.

This time when I awoke from surgery, I knew precisely why the doctor called it "major." He meant major pain. I also understood why stirring up my insides was characterized as exploratory. It felt like he pulled out my intestines and took a hike on them. I won't go on about this, but the most important thing was they could not detect any signs of cancer in the abdominal area. My cancer regimen would now turn to radiation and chemotherapy.

Please allow me to respectfully invite you to play my part as a first-time radiation recipient. Remember, being blind, you will not see your hospital surroundings at all. And yet, I think you will find, as I did, your predicament will become more vividly clear than you would want.

First, upon arriving within the hospital's nuclear medicine center, you would take a seat in the waiting room, and eventually hear your name called. You would leave your husband, your wife or your friend in the waiting area, and step forward with white cane open to clearly identify yourself as blind. You ask if you might take the arm of your calling technician, and then gently latch on as soon as the tech has done his or her about-face for the walk back down the hall toward the radiation treatment area. There, you are asked to disrobe and drape yourself in one of those stylish hospital gowns. It's the kind that invariably has one tie strap missing halfway down your backside. You hold it together awkwardly behind you, not just out of embarrassment, but for warmth, as you are then escorted across to the radiation therapy room.

Although you cannot see the room's immediate decor, you sense by the surrounding openness that the room is filled with cold, hard surfaces. Above your head, you notice a broad openness of sound and airy space as you walk. From this, you know that the ceiling is not within easy reach, and thus you can assume this is in order to accommodate the massive machines used for treatments.

Momentarily, your technician diverts your attention to introduce you to two other techs, each focused on their responsibilities and tasks at hand. But it's still the idea of the machine that gets your fullest attention. Soon, you are lying down on an icy metal table, with an unseen, presumably bulky steel artillery piece suspended over your body. Its name alone, linear accelerator, is intimidating. As you lie flat on your back on a table that feels impeccably solid, no doubt a part of the monster machine itself, you hear and feel one of the technicians lean under the monster and spread a sheet over you for warmth, and then a heavy lead blanket that covers your waist down almost to your knees to protect your ability to father children in the future. From there, an audibly low-pitched nuclear gun painlessly zaps you, staying within extremely precise lines. Radiation is first directed to the lymph gland system at your gut and then moves higher up to your neck.

But it doesn't stop there. Like a fish being broiled under intense heat, you are then turned over and radiated on the back side of the neck and up the back side of the head. As you continue to listen with eyes closed the nuclear gun continues blasting away.

The process lasts around ten minutes. As to any anxiety or discomfort you may have anticipated or feared in these treatments, you are pleasantly surprised with the ease in which your body accepts the cell-killing onslaught that is going on. This is so, in part, because like an X-ray, the radiation wastes no time in tearing through you at the speed of light. And instead of pain, you feel a strange sense of pleasure because now, more than any other time in life, you are at the center of attention of complete strangers. They are 100% focused on you. You are, in fact, in the spotlight. Your celebrity status, however, will be a short-lived joy.

It's only at the third or fourth treatment that you begin to feel the cumulative effects of far too much concentrated sun. Like the burn you would feel from placing your hand inside a working microwave oven, the burn from the linear accelerator in your throat and gut areas would radiate outward from within. For me, this phenomenon showed up as increasingly tender rawness, like a bad sunburn painted onto the inside of my throat. Even swallowing water felt like gulping down a fist full of nails! And of course, you lose hair – but not all of it. The back of your neck and head becomes as bare as a baby's bottom.

If you truly had to take this all on yourself, I have no doubt you would inspire everyone around you with your ability to tolerate such indignities. How do I know this? Because tolerance would be your only choice, just as it was for me.

After months of harsh struggles with not being able to keep down certain foods, fried foods in particular, radiation finally ended. Unfortunately, it ended in failure. Before it was even time for my scheduled sixth-month checkup, a brand new lump appeared – this time, it was behind my ear. *Now what? Does this mean I no longer have a "90% chance of cure?"* I dared not even speak the words aloud. I only knew that chemotherapy was no longer a backup. It was now my only remaining option.

The oncologist explained the procedure when we arrived for my first treatment. His voice was calm and reassuring. Perhaps it was that way because it was not he who was about to be filled with toxic chemicals!

He told us that he would insert a needle into a vein in my arm or into the top surface of my hand. He would then flood my veins with the chemical, sending throughout my body what he characterized as "a cool water sensation." He spoke to me as I lay in front of him. "David, after this injection, we'll need you to rest quietly for twenty minutes or so."

What came next was far beyond my expectation. The taste hit my tongue like a spoonful of pure mercury. The so-called "cool" feeling threw me into a violent retching. I rolled over like a kicked log. Vomit gushed out toward Connie. Everything – I mean everything within me – poured to the floor.

As Connie and the doctor used the nearby sink to wet paper towels and clean up the mess, I lay on the table for the full twenty minutes, my retching having halted temporarily. For a young man and his wife who had never experienced anything like this before, it was frightening new territory. Drenched in a cold sweat, I felt a sense of overwhelming dread. It was the awful realization that this was just the beginning. The doctor comforted us the best he could with his reassuring mild manner. At the same time, he turned and reminded his receptionist, "Dorothy? Can you hear me? Be sure and schedule David Meador for one week from today, same time next Friday."

I staggered out of the office with Connie, all the time pressing my hand against her lower back, white cane in the other, as we entered the elevator and both cringed at the thought of returning. It took us 30 minutes to drive home in the Chicago afternoon traffic. By the time we got to our apartment, I was feeling sick again – very sick. I vomited just about every hour for the first four hours, and then a few more times during the night. I remained weak and sick through Saturday, but by Sunday morning, I began to feel like joining Connie at our small kitchen table for meals.

Connie and I returned to our jobs Monday morning, not

saying anything to anyone about the awful Friday and Saturday we had just experienced. Fellow workers surely must have asked their usual Monday morning question, "How was your weekend?" How to answer? "Okay, I guess." For the life of me, I cannot remember explaining or saying anything more. Connie was employed as a teacher two bus rides away from our apartment. As for me, I was within walking distance of my office. But the difference between our worlds at that moment and those of our co-workers was immense. True, we were all very busy with our jobs. But perhaps more to the point, in my case, at age 24, I just did not have the words or the maturity to know how to breach this topic. It was safer, in my opinion, to just keep it to myself.

We repeated this Friday, Saturday and Sunday pattern for the first six weeks of treatments. Then, mercifully, chemotherapy visits spread out to once a month. Eventually, they decreased to one weekend a quarter. By the time Year Four came around, they were only every six months.

At the end of that year, my treatments were finally complete. Unfortunately there were complications under the surface, latent, not to show up again for a full ten years. But for now, Connie and I were overjoyed and thankful to have this difficult chapter come to a close.

# CHAPTER 8

## GRADUATE SCHOOL

M ost people don't obsess over the dangers of catching a subway train. But if you're a person traveling without sight, you really can't afford not to.

The subway in Chicago is known as the "L." Miles of rails map their way independently from the outlying cityscape to a circular route around the business district called the "Loop." Elevated rails and platforms downtown and throughout the city are at least twenty feet high, and for a blind person, each platform introduces a different theater of unknowns.

Underground, the height of platforms isn't so bad, but other concerns rise up in the roar. When you get off a train underground, you step into a cavern of concrete and echoes. Noise levels alternate between gripping and deafening. And when the rumble of your departing train is loudest, you have to stand perfectly still. Why? Because with the noise being so disorienting, just one misstep can cause you to fall face forward off the most dangerous diving board you will ever encounter. And if you should happen to land on the high voltage source called "the third rail," you're finished.

Traveling blind, you negotiate every step. Regardless of whether in the city or outlying neighborhoods, above ground or below, when waiting for the train, you must walk gingerly toward the platform's edge, all the time keeping your cane on the surface underfoot. You are wary of the freefall that you would experience if you stumbled off the edge and onto the track. And the same perils await you on your trip back home. Even if you are familiar with your gangplank, people standing with you ready to board the train will gasp as you white-cane your way directly over to the precipice.

Why walk towards the dangerous edge like that? You'd think I'd want to stay away from it at all times. This would be good thinking, except for one thing. When you're blind, it's essential you make the critical unknowns known. Unless you have the good fortune of receiving help from a sighted traveler, you need to locate those edges. You need to know in advance where the heck your train is going to pull up. You need to know where the doors will be because you'll only have a few seconds to find the opening and jump aboard.

If the train operator decides to stop your car twenty paces past you, you are facing a problem. You'd better be familiar with your danger line and be ready to scoot, because he won't wait. And if the need to scoot arises, you are far better off knowing the whereabouts of your platform's edge. Otherwise, you are frantically fox trotting across an unfamiliar dance floor in the direction of the train and an unknown step-off. You must use your head to find your best path, ignoring the audible inhales of onlookers. But just because you can successfully navigate the subway, that doesn't mean the city streets don't have their own surprises waiting around the bend.

One afternoon in the fall of 1974, I stood atop an elevated platform in our neighborhood on the Northwest Side, waiting patiently for a train that would take me to the Loop. I was going on what promised to be an adventure, and once again, it would be a promise fulfilled.

Sitting in my steel serpent as it jitterbugged south down the tracks, I listened through the train's half-opened windows to the wind and city rushing by. The trackside tenements and office buildings echoed back at us as we rattled by at top speed.

Several minutes into my ride, I could feel the train lean downward as we plunged into the cool underground just a mile or two from downtown. Our linked-up boxes soon reached a curve. The wheels squealed in the reverberating tunnel and threw off sparks and the smell of burning steel. I lurched slightly forward in my seat as the train operator hit the brakes and announced my Chicago Avenue stop.

When the doors opened, I scrambled out with the other exiting passengers. In the midst of one of the best examples of an echo chamber you can imagine, I listened closely for every audible clue. As soon as the din from our departing train faded away, the downtown station regained its composure. Keeping the tip of my cane sliding across the cement, I acted the part of a beagle puppy and followed the sound of shuffling footsteps toward the stairs and up to the fresh air above.

Once at the surface of the city, I knew my way. In alternating sun and shadows, I walked confidently with buildings on my right and city streets on my left. I tap-tap-tapped my cane south to Chicago Avenue and waited for the light. As it turned green, the traffic on my left surged straight up the street and gave me my signal to proceed. Taking special care to listen for traffic that might be turning into my crosswalk from behind or ahead, I reached my cane forward and tapped it rapidly to the other side.

Safely up on the opposite curb, I pivoted 90 degrees to the left as best I could. Hesitating long enough for the light to change, I then proceeded across my second street and continued east toward Lake Michigan. As I hurried to approach the next corner, I reminded myself I only had a few minutes to make my appointment. I stutter-stepped at the light, and then zoomed across.

As I scooted my white cane out to touch the curb on the other side, I immediately panicked. The tip of my cane hit absolutely nothing, just an abundance of air. Instinctively, everything about me tightened. My body seemed to lean, and then hover, over whatever open gap I was encountering. But I had no way to stop my momentum. All I could do was try to keep myself perfectly vertical as I dropped.

How would you feel if you were in my shoes, plunging off the world map without warning? Instantly, your spinal cord would flash several frantic messages to your brain: "What are we jumping into? A manhole? An open storm gutter? The Chicago River?!?"

My fall didn't last much more than a second, but it seemed like twenty. When I hit bottom, only my head, shoulders and upper chest were visible above the ground. I stood almost four feet down in a newly dug grave-size hole. Apparently, it had been left by a city crew excavating beneath the pavement's surface. I stood there motionless at the bottom in a state of shock.

A gentleman in his car at the intersection saw me as I crossed. He must have gasped as I leapt into that hole. Mayor Daley's lawyers no doubt would have called that hole "Liability Central" had I been the litigious type. Apparently I had threaded a perfect path through several orange and white barricades. From my new vantage point, I delivered a loud invective of seven words, "Who the hell left this hole here?!"

The man jumped out of his car and ran over to me. He reached down and took my cane and briefcase. In the meantime, I got a foothold on something and hoisted myself out. This concerned man and I stood together just a few seconds, both of us rattled, working to brush the dirt off my pants and sports coat. He then guided me out of this construction site and to the nearby sidewalk that would quickly lead me to my urgent downtown appointment.

During the preceding winter, I had evaluated my situation and determined that I wanted something different. Now that I had achieved my college dream of getting a good job with Bankers Life and Casualty, and having fought to keep it during my illness, it was time for a change. Isn't that the way it goes? Once we have what we want, we want something else.

Three years interviewing and recruiting at Bankers Life taught me a great deal, but I began to realize it wasn't going to get me anywhere. Connie and I talked about my grievances and my options. She agreed I should look at moving ahead; a step that we thought should involve graduate school. We looked into a Counseling Master's program, but realized counseling would be like interviewing and thus limiting the big dream.

The big dream? I was still hooked on memories of my father. He eventually became regional sales manager for the bottled gas company he had long worked for. During my early teen years, he shared with me sets of audio tapes produced by one of the most recognizable business motivational speakers of the time. This was the radio personality Earl Nightingale, a man who is memorialized to this day by the Nightingale-Conant Company of Chicago. Mr. Nightingale produced short motivational radio programs for nationally syndicated broadcasts. One of his sayings had stayed with me through the years, a saying that spoke to a person's potential rather than his or her worth. He declared that the minerals in our bodies might be appraised at only a dollar or two, but our value as creative thinkers is worth millions! With my hard-working dad as my example, I knew that I could excel in a career that was better suited to my capabilities, one that would allow me the chance to access those potential millions.

Connie and I chose a well-recognized graduate program at Loyola University. Loyola offered a Master's Degree in Personnel and Industrial Relations, the business of labor negotiations. I knew nothing of the past two centuries' epic American labor movement, a social upheaval that gave us a middle class that literally built the America we have today. I was unaware of Franklin D. Roosevelt's 1935 creation of the National Labor Relations Board, still the governing body for federal labor law. And I was oblivious to the legal requirement for federal mediation to curtail strikes in industries like health care, interstate trucking, rail, and other sectors essential to public safety. But I soon learned all of this and more once I was accepted to Loyola and I began the next chapter of my adult life.

Facing a new environment and a new set of challenges, that old feeling of panic set in again. Six weeks before my first term, I knew I needed to come up with a system for handling a high volume of on-site research in Labor Relations, Organizational Development, and Labor Law. My college strategy of having textbooks tape-recorded in advance would need to be upgraded, as the Loyola professors could be counted on to assign serious reading at the last moment. I would need a strategy that was more flexible, versatile, and immediate.

In the 1970s, the most innovative invention for reading text for the blind was an electronic scanning device called the Opticon. It was slightly larger than a cigar box and its maze of circuitry was concealed under a hard plastic cover. Not as hidden was its sticker price: $2,700.

Next to the purchase of our first car, a new Chevrolet Vega, this was our biggest expenditure to date. And yet, this new electronic reading aid captured my attention with its enticing promise of the freedom to read textbooks, newspapers, and even the mail without any outside assistance.

The Opticon sales representative met with Connie and me in our North Side apartment. Together, we sat at our dining room table. At first, the device surprised me with its simplicity. Curling out of the Opticon was a 24-inch cord with a fingertip-sized camera at the end. The idea was to have the user employ his or her hand to push the camera from left to right across any line of the printed page. The electronic eye would pick up each word, letter by letter.

So my right hand guided the camera slowly across a line of an open book sitting on the table in front of me. My left hand and fingers rested palm down inside the Opticon box, which sat just to the left. But here's where the "rubber met the road."

While my adroit hand slowly rolled the camera across a single letter, my left index finger felt the back-and-forth movement of a tingling shape within the box. The shivering form came from a grid of tiny vibrating pins representing the letter or word being scanned. You could actually feel the straight lines and curves of each letter vibrating and sliding under your fingertip. If you kept the camera inching forward, letters and words would glide under your finger like a New York Stock Exchange ticker tape. Clear to the touch? Yes, but it took concentration. And I knew it would take practice.

My first try proved both encouraging and daunting. It took me five full minutes to figure out the first letter. I eventually felt the fat capital D quivering under my finger. It was as though I was seeing the letter in my head – at least, it looked this way after the sales rep told me what the letter was. It took another five minutes to figure out the entire first word.

You might think my falling in love with this new technology was shortsighted. But I had not seen a single familiar letter of the alphabet in years. This package of electronics represented a fantastic hope – the hope that I could regain something essential, something I thought I had lost forever. What else would an excited young couple do in our situation? We bought!

Just weeks before the fall term, my pressing need was to read with speed. Nothing super-sonic, 60 words a minute would suffice. Slow reading, one letter at a time, was of course frustrating. But then – Eureka! – I discovered that Opticon training was to be offered at a nearby university. There I would get the training and expertise needed to let me read the printed page. Excited? Yes! The opportunity to learn how to use this miracle machine to its fullest extent excited me to no end! I could not wait!

So on a Monday morning, Connie drove me to the north-south Regional Railway commuter station and I took a train a few miles north to the university. The campus training center was surprisingly quiet. I got there at 9:00 a.m. as requested, but there was no receptionist. In fact, I didn't hear anyone in the building at all. In doubt whether I was even in the right place, I simply waited.

In a few minutes, the receptionist showed up and assisted me to the training room. Excitedly, I fired up the Opticon and began to read the first word on the first page of my user manual without much progress. The receptionist said she expected my trainer, a young lady named Elaine, any time. Opening the hinged crystal on my watch, I felt for the time with my index finger every ten minutes or so.

My trainer finally walked in at 10:20, well over an hour late, and offered no apology whatsoever. She asked without embarrassment, "Are you waiting for someone?" "I think I'm waiting for you," I said, still hoping we could salvage the morning. She hung up her coat, got a cup of coffee, and sat down with me. I was angry and hurt. She had absolutely no idea how essential, how imperative, how crucial this class was to me. Nor did she know how much of an emotional and monetary investment I put into this device.

As I started to explain my desperate desire to make this contraption work for me, the telephone rang. Not at all catching my tone, my so-called teacher picked up the phone from her desk and began talking. It was her boyfriend. She put him on hold and went to an adjacent room to talk in private. After twenty more minutes of waiting, I saw my highly anticipated three hours of training begin to circle the drain. By now, I realized I was supposed to meet Connie at the commuter station in just 90 minutes. This young woman wasn't offering anything. And unfortunately, neither was my expensive miracle machine.

Expectations dashed, I began crying silently, tears glazing my cheeks. I couldn't help it. This was the first time I cried since I was a child. Even my loss of sight did not bring me to tears. But now this piercing disappointment welled up in me all at once.

I sat at my table and continued giving it my best on my own. I guided the bug-like camera with my right hand over the first letter of the first word of the magazine article my instructor had apparently laid out for me. My left index finger could barely sense the tingle as I moved the camera across the bold first letter over and over again. Struggling with a lump in my throat, I realized this $2,700 contraption would never work, at least not for me. Perhaps it would make a good doorstop. At the very least, I knew I would not be able to read cases at the law library in just a few weeks.

A few days later, I found out I was mercifully very wrong. Miracle of miracles: It turned out I would soon receive hundreds of hours of help in one of the busiest business environments in the world – Downtown Chicago. But this time, there would be no electronic wiring, just a powerful connection with something far better – people who cared.

I learned from a friend that an agency of volunteer readers was available downtown near the Loyola campus. The agency was called the Blind Service Association, a privately funded group that had been assisting blind people in Chicago since 1924. Eager to see if they could help me, I contacted them to set up an appointment. When the day arrived, I took the subway and met the director, Ms. Beatrice Fredman, at her office. Ms. Fredman was a lovely lady in her 50s. She spoke with a certain confidence, and with good reason. An accomplished actress in the Chicago theater scene, Ms. Fredman would later earn roles in movies like *Four Friends* and *Field of Dreams*.

In a matter of days, Ms. Fredman introduced me to a special volunteer: Mr. Maury Letz, a downtown attorney who was willing to walk over twice a week to read the day's news as it relates to the history of labor law. What a find. What a service! What a testimony to the generosity of already busy people.

On Tuesdays and Fridays, Mr. Letz stretched his regular lunch hour to spend two full hours with me at the Blind Service Association's suite of offices downtown. Having an experienced Chicago lawyer available to help me read articles from the Chicago Tribune or Chicago Sun Times was a privilege beyond my wildest dreams. Compared to feeling for one quivering letter at a time, Mr. Letz's reading confirmed the obvious. Nothing reads like a good pair of eyes, especially when connected to an educated brain. This generous attorney continued to read to me throughout the latter half of the summer and a week or two into my classes in the fall.

Course requirements, however, quickly highlighted my need for an additional reader. My growing challenge was for someone to accompany me for on-site research in the Loyola University library. One of my professors assigned my class the job of reading and summarizing a weekly list of landmark Supreme Court cases. Unlike textbooks, these volumes were cases scattered throughout the University library. But where could I find a person to spend hours with me in the library?

To my relief, Ms. Fredman of BSA answered the question. She suggested another delightful reading catch, a highly educated sophisticate named Mrs. Barbara Cady. Mrs. Cady was a world-class reader. She was a stylish woman – a widow and a devoted mother to her grown children, she was even a member of the Chicago Yacht Club. She knew everyone and loved to talk about the latest news or the weather, or whatever it was you put in front of her – including the written page.

Mrs. Cady was in her early 70s and possessed boundless energy. Meeting at the library twice a week, she would read to me three hours at a time, allowing me to interrupt every five minutes or so to ask her to back up and read a certain paragraph again. Plowing through ten or fifteen Supreme Court cases each meeting, Mrs. Cady would sit patiently as I used a portable tape recorder to capture the important parts of each assigned case. And when we were finished, she would haul that particular stack of books back to the racks, and return with an equally heavy pile of others. Our meetings lasted for the better part of two years.

Best of all, Mrs. Cady fell in love with me. I don't mean romantically. She loved our every appointment, our every conversation on the phone or in person, our every reading marathon in the law library basement. And you know what? I *fell* in love with her, too.

Why else would I have run so recklessly across that downtown Chicago street on a sunny fall afternoon? And why would I have broken my own safety rules, ending up chest-deep in that construction hole? The truth is, there was an extremely important person waiting for me just one block beyond my leap.

Mrs. Cady and I relished both our time together and our achievements. Like the Fourth of July, my graduation day was to both of us "Independence Day." She proudly joined Connie and me at my Loyola ceremony. After all, it was Mrs. Cady who helped make it possible.

Barbara Cady was more than just a friend and a reader. Her inspiration, commitment, and devotion to me made her a lady worth falling for.

LOYOLA UNIVERSITY awarded 1,975 degrees during dual commencement ceremonies June 12 at McCormick Place. Above, David F. Meador (center), who is blind, is congratulated by Father Raymond C. Baumhart, S.J., Loyola president, upon receiving his master of science degree in industrial relations. Looking on at right is Alan J. Fredian, director of Loyola's Institute of Industrial Relations. *New World Photo*

*Article from a Chicago newspaper, June 1976*

# CHAPTER 9

# BECOMING A SOUTHERNER

Back in college, Connie and I had decided that if we could live in any city, it would be Nashville. It was our dream city, the perfect place to live and raise a family. Admittedly, our musings were partly driven by our TV habits of the time, watching the Glen Campbell and Johnny Cash programs. And some of those habits continued into the beginning of our married lives.

A few months before our first wedding anniversary, during a particularly cold Chicago spring, we decided to see if Nashville's reality could match our dream. While we were still enticed by the music, it was Chicago's cold weather more than Nashville's Country music that drove us to seek out the Southern sun in our first spring as a married couple. And so, at last, we gave ourselves the honeymoon we had delayed, and there discovered ourselves and our future.

We selected an especially romantic style of conveyance. Traveling by rail, a Pullman sleeping car would slowly rock us down to Tennessee's Music City.

The Illinois Central departed downtown Chicago at 9:00 in the evening. In no time, it crept through the southern half of the city and out of town. We lay snug in our upper berth and watched the bright lights of Chicago slowly fade into distant flickerings.

Our slumber car rambled its way by many familiar Central and Southern Illinois small towns as we slept through the night. We woke up hours later to gaze out our Pullman car window and admire a soft Kentucky dawn and its pastoral scenery of white fences and thoroughbred horses. They posed out on the misty green grass like a serene painting.

Three hours later, our train rumbled confidently into a bright Nashville morning. We stepped off the train and admired the bus-

tling yet quaint commercial site that would later be transformed
into one of the city's most unique and modern hotels, Nashville's
Union Station. However, in the spring of 1972, it was just a noisy
and teeming train depot.

Early the next day, Connie and I boarded a bus for a Gray Line
tour. One stop took us to The Hermitage, the storied and stately
home of our nation's seventh president, Andrew Jackson, and his
wife, Rachel. We strode hand in hand among the tulip poplars
lining the long driveway in front of the presidential mansion, and
browsed through each room listening to the learned commentary
of volunteer guides. We were tourists, yet we felt as if we were
longtime friends of the Jacksons and wished we could someday

return. That evening, we capped off a magical day with a trip to the legendary Grand Ole Opry.

When not visiting one of Nashville's many historic sites, or enjoying its wonderful southern cooking, we sat poolside in the warm Tennessee sun. Our last day brought a fun photo opportunity. Connie and I had an hour or so to while away before heading to the train station, so we browsed through a touristy store that carried Western wear. Connie put a cowboy hat on my head and took my photograph right there next to the rack. This picture said it all. It showed me sporting a big smile, a sunburned face, and a signature Music City look. This would remain a memorable snapshot of our trip, and a reminder of our long-held dream to one day live there.

That very day would arrive about four years later. After I finished my cancer treatments and graduate school, we decided to give our dream city a real try. The question was how to approach this giant task, which would involve another tedious job search for me.

A few months before completing Loyola's Masters program, Connie and I decided to rely on our proven job-hunting methods of the past. From our Chicago apartment, Connie helped me get out letters to the major employers in Nashville. But unlike our letter campaign five years earlier, this time we found absolutely no takers.

What to do? I decided to fly down alone to see if I'd have better luck in person. A show of independence might be impressive. "Connie," I said, "trust me, something good is bound to happen." I planned to visit those employers to whom I had written. Because if something good was indeed going to happen, it needed to happen soon.

One of the flight attendants led me off the plane and into the Nashville airport. The gate agent called a skycap for me. My skycap then guided me to baggage claim, retrieved my bags, and showed me out to catch a cab. I tipped him three dollars, a big tip in those days. Why? Because his service at that moment made him more important to me than the President of the United States.

I checked into a motel downtown, and early the next morning I began phoning several of the personnel directors on my list. In almost every instance, none of these people were available to take my call, so I left messages all over the city. After phoning all of my contacts, I had no choice but to hit the streets.

I phoned for a taxi and headed towards the business district, which was not quite like Chicago's but was exciting nonetheless. Sitting in the back seat, I pulled out of my briefcase my Braille list of those twenty or so major employers of interest, and dictated the top half to the driver. He took me to the closest one – the University of Tennessee's Nashville campus.

The head of personnel there was Bob Craighead, PhD. Dr. Craighead told me that he was sorry, but he had nothing available. However, he offered to make a contact for me at Vanderbilt University. He picked up the phone, the man on the other end said come right over, and the next thing I knew, Dr. Craighead was insisting on driving me there.

I was shocked at this display of kindness, which felt far different from Chicago. We arrived at the prestigious Vanderbilt campus within ten minutes. Bob introduced me to the head of a department; I cannot remember which one. He then stepped out and waited in the nearby reception room.

The department head, a man of about 40, opened our interview by asking me to lead us in prayer. This was definitely *not* Chicago. I felt "on the spot," especially as a Catholic boy who knew no spoken prayers except for the Our Father and Hail Mary, but I gave it my best shot. "Dear God, I thank You for this chance to be in Nashville, and for this interview, and *(gulp)* for the job offer I hope will be coming." It wasn't.

Bob took me to lunch, and then offered to drive me back to the business district. Earlier, I had asked him about three large downtown banks that had been on my list, so he drove me to that area. Business people and state government workers employed at the nearby Capitol Building walked across streets, and in and out of crosswalks all around. As we crawled along in the slow traffic, Bob offered a commentary on our surroundings. He described what buildings we were passing, and how the upcoming banks would all be within walking distance of each other.

He stopped the car on Fifth Avenue in front of the first bank to let me out. "Bob, I can't thank you enough," I said with genuine gratitude as I quickly shook his hand and began to open the car door. Once outside, I sat my briefcase down and leaned in toward the passenger side window. "Bob!" I raised my voice a few decibels over the noise around us. "I'll call and let you know what happens." I was alone in Nashville, but thanks to Bob, I did not feel lonely.

Picking up my briefcase, I walked away from his car, and did my best to follow his suggestion and cast off in a perpendicular direction. The din of traffic bounced back at me from the nearby buildings. I kept my shoulders square to stay on the straight course Bob had recommended. Once I neared my destination, the obvious absence of sound beyond the building's gigantic exterior directly ahead revealed its massive presence. Hitting the building's front entrance with my cane, I sidestepped left until I found the vertical metal handle and opened the door. Once inside, someone showed me up the elevator to Personnel.

The lady in the personnel office told me all she could do was pass along my resume. I had no choice but to thank her, leave the resume, and ask if she could take a moment to show me out. Exiting the elevator, I asked her to point me in the direction of another bank just up the street.

I then made my way a block north, crossed a couple of streets and found the next bank's entrance with the help of two pedestrians. It took me a little while to locate a security guard, who then showed me to the correct office. Soon, a young lady about my age escorted me into her office. "Mr. Meador, what job are you seeking?" she asked. What came to mind is the same quip that hundreds of job applicants in Chicago must have uttered under their breath to me at Bankers Life. "Hmm. How about yours?"

I soon began to recognize that personnel department opportunities within any bank in Nashville might be few and far between. Unlike in Chicago, where applicant interviewing duties required upwards of six interviewers, this was not the case in the smaller Nashville community banks. I soon made my way out to the street and headed in a new direction.

The bank guard showed me across Union Street and instructed me to walk two blocks east toward the Cumberland River. This led me toward my next prospect, the city government office located in the Stahlman Building. On my Braille list was the name of the Metropolitan Government personnel director to whom I had written earlier.

With a little guidance from someone out front, I entered through both sets of glass doors and walked into the building. The elevator and its bell spoke out to me immediately. I shuffled my way toward the open elevator, careful to avoid colliding with my fellow passengers. A lady offered her assistance as she moved past me to catch the closing door. She kindly pushed the button in response to my request for the second floor.

As the doors opened, I instantly heard the echoing sounds of heavy marble corridors extending to my left, right, and straight ahead. As I white-caned my way down the hall in front of me, I could easily hear busy office workers typing and talking through open doors on either side. At the end of the hallway, I heard the voice of what I imagined to be a pretty receptionist. My cane bumped over a threshold noticeably changing the surface beneath me from marble to carpet.

The receptionist was on the phone. I took three short steps forward and touched the bottom of her desk with my cane. Waiting until she finished answering her caller's questions, I introduced myself and asked if Mr. Joe Huggins was available. She was slightly taken aback by the sight of me with my cane. "Please have a seat," she stammered. I did so, and waited.

"Mr. Huggins will see you now," she announced after a few short minutes, and then displayed a courage and sensitivity I did not expect. She walked around her desk and offered her elbow. "Please take my arm," she said, "I'll show you back to his office." At first Mr. Huggins sounded like he was playing a theatrical part. His character seemed fresh off a Mississippi plantation. "I am so pleased to meet you, David," Mr. Huggins said. "Let me show you to a seat."

This director of personnel proved to be completely genuine. He told me he remembered my letter, and that he was impressed I would fly alone to Nashville. It probably helped that I was from downstate Illinois and thus sounded a little Southern myself. He soon called into his office the two personnel department supervisors under his dispatch. We all got along splendidly as they asked detailed questions about my graduate degree, abilities and goals. I loved the sound and attitude of these people, and was thrilled with the good fortune of my timing.

Shockingly, I was hired on the spot! I felt like yelling "Bingo!" right there in front of Mr. Huggins and his two employees! I was ecstatic! Sure, this new job might be a lot like the one I had in Chicago, but it was a big, big change, one that would allow Connie and me to make our Nashville dream a reality.

Here I was, back in Nashville just a few years after our initial visit with a solid new job lined up. I stood warm and toasty at an outdoor phone booth explaining to Connie – who was stuck of course in cold and blustery Chicago – my good fortune and the details of the job offer.

"Honey," I blurted out, "I told you something good would happen. We've done it! I've got a job!" I just had to string it out a bit. "First, I want you to know I failed flat as a pancake with the universities. And also with the banks. I met a really good man in the middle though, named Bob Craighead. But you know what? We got our break with the Metropolitan Government of Nashville!" Of course, I gave my wonderful wife a chance to ask some questions. But then I could not help but interrupt and continue with exuberance. "We have done it, and they want me to start on the first of July!" Finally, Connie got in a word edgewise. "David, are you sure we should really do this?" She began to bring me back to reality. It was true – moving south would mean Connie would have to walk away from her work and all of her relationships there. I, too, would be giving up my hard-earned familiarity with the Chicago subway and our neighborhood, as well as our favorite broadcast stations, restaurants, and sports teams. And I would be turning away from whatever career momentum I had with Bankers Life. I felt a deep loyalty for the people there who gave me my start, my first job. And so, Connie repeated her wise and reasonable question, "Should we really give up what we have here?"

We listened to one another on the phone, each pondering what the other was truly thinking. Suddenly, the feel, sound and smell of springtime in Tennessee overwhelmed me. "Connie," I said, "don't you remember how gorgeous it is here? The warmth of the sun, the birds singing in the trees all around. I just wish you were here to see it." Connie's mind and heart seemed to transport her instantly to my side. She replied with exuberant resolve, "Okay, David, let's go for it! Let's become Southerners!"

We knew, of course, that acclimating ourselves to a different region of the country meant we had to keep a pretty open mind. For one thing, Connie and I would have to learn an expanded form of American English. My first lesson came directly from my new boss.

My first day on the job, a department supervisor – Barry Jones – invited me to join him and his friend Richard for lunch. Barry was one of the supervisors who had backed me wholeheartedly during the interview and hiring process. He soon became one of my very best friends. He offered to "carry" us across the bridge over the Cumberland River to Captain Apollo's fried fish restaurant. "Carry me and Richard across the bridge?" I asked, "What do you mean?"

He answered my query quickly. "Look," Barry said, "this is something we do all the time. We go to Apollo's on the other side of the river at least twice a week. How else are you going to get there, David?" "But you're going to carry us across the river?" I asked. I thought about saying, "Seems like carrying two of us across the bridge would be a bit heavy for you, Barry." But I abruptly realized what he meant as the three of us jumped into Barry's pickup and "got carried" across the bridge.

Barry knew I was a fellow golfer and thus immediately saw me as a friend. Luckily for me, he soon had an opening in his regular foursome and asked me to join them for their early tee time each and every Saturday morning. And with me on board, we made for quite an interesting crew. One of Barry's golfing buddies, Virgil, was a case study in Southern character who proved to be very memorable. Lanky, tall and always playing the role of an exaggerated country type, Virgil swaggered around and spoke from a storehouse of one-liners to draw from at any moment. Though he was only 60, he often referred to himself as old. Without the slightest reduction in confidence, "Old Virgil" creaked and groaned as he warmed up his golf club on the first tee. He looked over at me after his last warm-up swing and said, "David, they say when you get older, the legs are the first to go." Virgil was also something of a ladies man. "Don't you believe it about the legs," he quipped.

By sheer coincidence, we moved to Nashville the same year – 1976 – that the United States Blind Golf Association National Championship was to be held in the city. My dad came all the way down from Illinois to coach me in the tournament. We ended up quite pleased with our fifth place finish in a field of 25 golfers – especially since this was only our third try. As great as it was to have Dad in town and on the course with me, we both knew he wouldn't be able to make every tournament, let alone have any time to practice together, so we put out word that I was looking for a coach. Dad was still in town when I received a call introducing Stuart Smith as a prospective coach.

A friend of Stuart's father, who had caught a brief segment on the local evening news about our national tournament, had referred him to me. Seeing the impressive caliber of golf being played and learning that I was looking for a coach, he had immediately thought of Stuart. Stuart was a high school junior and a notable player in his own right. A meeting was quickly arranged for the next evening at one of the city's municipal courses, Harpeth Hills. This youngster showed a special flair from the moment we met.

Dad and I watched Stuart hit a drive off the first tee just before we were introduced. He sure looked like a golfer – five feet nine inches tall, 140 pounds. His hair was bleached blonde by the sun and he brandished a dark suntan from his hours on the course.

*David's father setting up a shot*

What's more, this high school kid could absolutely rocket the ball, farther than either my dad or I could come close to hitting.

"Mr. Meador," Stuart said politely, "why don't you let me see how you and your dad work together?" I felt a bit intimidated having to hit a golf ball for this young man. Dad set me up to the ball in our usual manner and asked that I go ahead and hit a drive down the fairway as Stuart had just done. I swung as well as Stuart had, but there was just one difference – I missed the ball altogether!

In the years since, Stuart has replayed his reaction to my first swing many times to friends. When telling the story, he quickly gets to his standard punch line, "And you know what Dave did? He whiffed it!" This always gets a laugh, especially when I'm present. Then Stuart follows with a sincere compliment to me, "And do you know what Dave did after that miss?" He pauses to let people see the twinkle in his eye. "Dave did absolutely nothing. He didn't laugh... he didn't curse... he didn't apologize... he didn't make any excuses. And with all the wisdom of a 16-year-old, I said to myself, here's a guy I can help." Little did we know that 30 years down the road, he and I would still be golfing together, this time along with his children and my grandchildren. Stuart has done much more than just help me play golf – he became someone with whom I've shared many a laugh and story with over the years, a true friend.

"Carry you across the bridge?" Indeed, my new Nashville friends made this happen for me. They carried me across the bridge, from a newly transformed city boy back to my roots as a small town nice guy. With their help, I went from someone who occasionally played golf to someone who played every weekend. They carried me from the past to a fulfilling present – from a big city of concrete and chaos to a smaller city offering green trees and a fresh new life.

As we all face inevitable changes in our lives, the key question is "how?" How will we handle changes in health, changes within our family, and changes where we live? My suggestion: Keep building friendships along the way. No matter what, no matter where, they will help you stay in the game.

# CHAPTER 10

# WINNING AT FIRESTONE

Early in life, I learned an important lesson. Golf can slice you with hurt if you are not ready for it, and sometimes even if you are.

I got my first taste of that hurt as a bright-eyed 10-year-old. My feelings were on the line. For the very first time, I offered myself up for hire. Job site: our local nine-hole country club. Expertise: golf caddy.

This was in 1958, before the popularization of electric carts. In those days, most people strapped their bag to a flimsy two-wheel pull-cart. If you wanted to elevate yourself from the commonplace, you could hire a caddy, a show of class and money.

I was about to start the fifth grade. Perhaps I was a bit young for employment, but I was eager to try. Besides, there were no other "baggers" around when my opportunity arrived. Swaggering Floyd Fox showed up on a Saturday morning with his foursome, well after the early golfers had teed off.

Floyd was a regular. He was a colorful dresser and a big-talking, self-anointed golf hotshot who walked with a rolling, rhythmic style, almost as though he had an extra set of knees. He played religiously every Saturday and Sunday, smoked a big cigar when doing so, and always wore a broad-brimmed hat tilted forward. I spotted Floyd striding toward the clubhouse from the parking lot, dressed in swank blue slacks, lighter blue shirt, and alligator golf shoes. I got up my nerve and called out, "Hey Floyd! Want a caddy?" I was unaware that a 10-year-old should not address an adult by first name. Thankfully, Floyd didn't seem to mind. And just like that, I had my first job.

Three holes into the round, I felt a sense of accomplishment for not struggling too much with carrying Floyd's large leather bag. Glowing with the pride that can come with partnership, I strode confidently at his side as we approached the fourth tee. Floyd didn't seem to share my good mood, as he was already down by three or four strokes.

It was then that Floyd pulled rank and told me to scrub up three of his golf balls. I took the balls he handed me and dutifully ran in the direction he pointed. The ball washer stood at the back of the tee. This strange contraption could not have been more imposing. It sat atop a pole and looked to me like an oversized milkshake mixer. Strangely, it had a smooth wooden handle sticking out the top. It stood about chest-high. As I pulled the wooden handle up, I saw that there was just enough room for a ball to be shoved down into a shaft filled with water. The mixer shaft was lined with scary stiff, wiry scrub brushes.

Confused and nervous, I hurriedly placed all three balls, one at a time, into the opening at the top. I used the vertical paddle to pound the balls, one after the other, down past the brushes into the grimy water. As I pulled the wet wooden paddle up for the last time, I was unsure what to do next. Only then did I notice that in the center lower portion of the board was a perfectly round hole – just the right size for a golf ball.

It was too late now, though. All three of Floyd's balls were lodged at the bottom between industrial strength brushes. My face flushed with embarrassment. I had no choice but to squeeze my hand down elbow-deep between the wire brushes to wrench the balls from the murky water. Mumbling a prayer for healing, I dried the balls on the hanging towel and ran them back to my employer.

I don't know if it was my crimson face or my flagging red hand, but Mr. Fox smiled, half embarrassed for me and half for him. I knew then that this would be a day I would not soon forget. I rationalized my situation with that most enduring and logical of questions: "What good is golf to anyone anyway?"

The next summer, I was caddying for my dad. He was paired with two golfers who played a game considerably better than his. These were the best golfers at our course – Dr. Whitten, a chiropractor, and Dr. Woods, a medical doctor.

This time, as a seasoned 11-year-old, I bent over and studiously peered down the line of my dad's long putt. Here on the third green, Dad needed to make this one to stay two strokes back of the doctors. Still bending over, I backed up for a better view. My feet got tangled up on a long-handled rake that was lying at the top of a sand trap. In full view of my dad and our club squires, I tumbled backwards, pancaking flush down in the trap on my butt. I held my position, imprinting my posterior in the sand. My legs and arms stretched courageously out toward my dad, as though I had just landed a record-breaking Olympic long jump. I was not, however, hearing any cheers from the crowd. Instead, silence. It was the silence of three grown men turning to hide their faces as they burst with laughter. I picked myself up, took three steps back up to the surface, looked carefully down the line, and said, "Breaks two balls to the left."

Okay, I'm lying about that part. I wish I had said it just that way. Instead, I dragged around all day and all month with the memory of falling backwards into that oversized sand box, burning with embarrassment. Once again, I coped with my situation by asking: "What good is golf to anyone anyway?"

This was the kind of mental baggage I brought with me when I first moved to Tennessee. Fortunately, my new young coach and my golf buddies taught me by example to set aside those emotional carry-ons. They loved the game, and they wanted me to be competitive within their foursome and with others. And so, my friend and boss, Barry, would pick me up early on Saturday mornings. We would drive to Harpeth Hills, a local municipal course, for a 7:00 a.m. tee time. Stuart would already be standing around the first tee with Mack and Virgil, ready to rock and roll.

Stuart, however, was not just a weekend player. A couple of late afternoons each week during that first summer together, my young coach would pick me up for our regular practice session. He would show up in his very first car, a roughed up Opel Manta two-seater, which he affectionately called a "beater" – as in "eggbeater" because of the way it sounded when he let off the clutch. I would have just arrived home from work, so I'd quickly change clothes to shorts and t-shirt, and off we would churn. We would then motor to a suburban park, the Edwin Warner Polo Grounds, and hit shots across a broad field of grass. Stuart would stride down this equestrian playground and collect all 50 or so of our practice balls, and then return for me to hit them again. Come Saturday morning, we would tee it up on the course with Barry and his friends for our weekly foursome. Stuart and I grew to become a pretty good team.

A little more than a year later, well practiced and with dozens of Saturday morning matches under our belts, Stuart and I flew

# Blind Golf Title Sought by Meador

**By JIMMY DAVY**

David Meador adopted Nashville as his new hometown sight unseen.

Meador, you see, is blind.

**BUT, HE HAS** a feeling for the warmth of the city and, because of it, gives Nashville a solid championship contender in the National Blind Golfers Tournament, this weekend at Firestone Country Club in Akron, O.

"My wife and I came to Nashville on vacation about five years ago and fell in love with the city. About 15 months ago we quit our jobs in Chicago and moved," Meador said. He now works for the Metropolitan government personnel department on test development and recruitment.

Meador moved here shortly after the national blind event was played at Hillwood in the summer of 1976. He is the fifth-ranked blind golfer in the country.

The only problem with moving, however, is that it is necessary to find a new coach — the guy who actually places the clubhead in position to strike the golf ball properly.

—Staff Photo by Frank Empson

**Blind golfer David Meador is joined by new coach, Stewart Smith, in a practice session for this weekend's National Blind Tournament at the Firestone Country Club in Akron, Ohio. With them is Meador's wife Connie.**

*Article from* The Tennessean *before the tournament, September 1977*

to Akron, Ohio for the 1977 United States Blind Golf Association National Championship at the prestigious Firestone Country Club.

Understand what a privilege this was. At the time, Firestone was the site of the nationally televised World Series of Golf, a select annual match involving only the winners of the highly esteemed "Majors" – the Masters, the U.S. Open, the British Open, and the PGA Championship. I remembered seeing this exalted course once or twice on TV in my mid-teens. Its fairways were an impressive deep emerald green. They flourished with the advantage of being watered all night with sprinklers. Firestone was unquestionably far superior to the sun-parched hills I grew up playing back home in Southern Illinois.

Arriving that first morning for practice on the Firestone layout, the atmosphere felt country-club rich. Sounds were few. The course lay ahead of us as quiet as a Civil War cemetery. Around several of the greens, the scent of well-tended flowerbeds graced the air. The grass was wet from overnight rains. Fairways were plush and covered in stretches with shallow standing water. Stuart must have felt like a kid out of school – which he was.

At the end of our practice round, Stuart let his youth show, to my delight. Guiding our golf cart down the 18th fairway across a film of water and gleaming wet grass, Stuart turned in tight doughnuts, spinning us in sloshy circles. It was as though we put our ride into a spin across the finish line like King Richard Petty at Daytona. Tomorrow, our driving would need to be all business, and *straight*.

On the first day of formal competition, we got off to a reasonable start, scoring a 103. Fortunately for us, very few of our three-dozen competitors did markedly better on this long and difficult par-70 south course. Stuart and I finished the day four strokes out of first place.

The second and concluding day, we were off to a worse start, finishing the front nine with a tepid 56. But on the back nine, things began to heat up. By the time we walked off the 15th green, we knew we were in contention. Our scorecard showed we were only one over bogey through the first six holes of a greatly improved back nine.

Now we had to face No. 16, the infamous "Monster Hole" at Firestone. It stretched out some 585 yards – the longest par-five on the course. My knees began to feel weak. We started with a sky-ball tee shot that went only 155 yards down the middle. My second shot, a well struck three-wood, soared 220 yards down the left side.

This was the real challenge. We were looking at another 210 yards to the pin, but we needed to carry the water on the front-right and avoid two bunkers at the back protecting the shallow green. One alternative would be to hit an iron just short of the water to leave us with a wedge shot up and onto the dance floor. But Stuart realized the strength of my game was in the longer shots, not the shorter pitching wedge lobs. He decided our best probability was not to baby up, but instead go for broke. He handed me a two-iron.

At the time, I was using a set of clubs handed down to me from my father years earlier. These were Jackie Burke "Punch-Irons," heavy and a load to swing, but they were up to the test. I absolutely jumped all over this shot. The ball launched toward the green. I knew I caught every bit of it. As soon as the ball missiled into the air, Stuart began begging it for more. "Get up!" he yelled. "Get up, get up!"

The ball hit a couple of steps past the far side of the water's edge. It bounced twice and scampered up onto the green just 24 feet to the right of the hole. This was a miracle shot, considering the pressure. Well really, for me, it was a miracle shot regardless. A two-iron was not the club I would expect to count on, but there it was. My heart leapt with joy. Fantastic – a 210-yard shot finishing only 24 feet from the stick! If I could get the ball down in two putts, this would give us a par on the Monster 16th.

I banged the first putt eight feet past the hole. Not so good. We took our time with the putt coming back. I visualized the distance as just one body length, plus two feet. I gave it the best stroke I could. The ball rolled toward the hole. I heard nothing – no word from Stuart, no ball hitting the bottom of the cup. Then, as I was about to heave a sigh of frustration, Stuart gave out a whoop as it toppled in! "Okay, okay, okay!" I yelled, and then quipped to Stuart, "Just another routine par at the Monster."

"Now we're on a roll," I predicted with confidence. "Not so fast," Stuart said to me as we strode to the next tee. He was right. I quadruple-bogeyed the 17th, leaving us two over bogey with one hole to go.

The 18th hole at Firestone is a par four dogleg to the left, measuring a long 435 yards to the flag. This finishing test thankfully begins from an elevated height. But the hole required a good drive in order to have any chance of reaching the dogleg. "Please, let me hit this last drive straight, and far," I prayed.

We hit a low line drive off the elevated tee. The ball rifled straight down the middle but stopped after traveling no more than 200 yards total, ending up somewhere short of the dogleg. Luckily, my second shot got up over the branches on the left, and landed on the right side of the fairway. No surprise, we still lacked 45 yards to the pin. We knew it was 45 yards exactly because Stuart paced it off, every step, all the way from my ball to the flag.

As he arrived back a little out of breath, my young coach informed me of the yardage and set me up to hit the kind of shot we had practiced many times at the Polo Grounds. It would take a nearly 70% swing with the sand wedge. Unfortunately, these short shots were not proving to be my forte in this tournament so far.

Throughout the day, an unconscious swing flaw had created a troublesome issue in my short game. Just a small thing, such as allowing the right knee to straighten on the downswing of a short swing, can be disastrous. The result is often a dreaded shank, with the ball going almost dead right. That's exactly what had happened twice, resulting in my quadruple bogey on No. 17.

"David, keep that right knee bent," I repeated under my breath. Stuart set me up to the ball in a resolute fashion. I've always contended that 90% of the swing is in the set-up. Knowing this, I took my time getting my body balanced over the ball.

Stuart knelt on one knee and held both shaft and clubface steady in perfect alignment to the green. I opened my hips to the target line, and placed most of my weight on my left side. This would get my left side out of the way and eliminate any sway in my swing. Still standing over the shot, I lowered my left shoulder down about three inches to assure a steeper angle up and then down through the swing. This would still allow both my left and right arms to remain fully extended through the hitting zone at the bottom.

Keeping my weight back on my heels, I bent both knees and kicked the right one toward the target to maintain that critical right knee position through the swing. Short-game checklist completed, I signaled Stuart with a word to back away: "Ready."

*Crinkle-swish-swish* came the rustling sounds of my clothing as I swung the club back to a pre-determined height. *Swish-click-pop!* The click of the clubface on the ball sounded good, but the silence coming from the little crowd of already finished blind players, coaches, and a few onlookers made me wonder. My guess was the ball was still in the air and had not yet landed. Then suddenly I heard a yell from our little crowd, and from Stuart, "Great shot!"

*David and Stuart Smith at Firestone Country Club, 1977*

Stuart wasted no time in getting us up onto the green, our official score keeper following us to the apron. My coach quickly walked me from the ball to the hole and back. "David, the distance is eighteen feet. What do you think?" "I believe it breaks a little to the left," I answered. Apparently, he saw the same line. My capable 17-year-old coach lined me up to a spot ten inches to the right, and told me to stroke the putt as though our distance was only twelve feet. The ball slowly fed downhill, curved left toward the hole, and then, dropped with a roar from the crowd! "Great read, Stuart!" I said, slapping him on the back. "A par on 18 – a fantastic finish to our national tournament," I boasted as we walked off the green.

We finished one over bogey, a cool 45, on the famous back nine at Firestone! "But wait," Stuart said guardedly. "We haven't won yet." Perennial reigning champion, Pat Browne of New Orleans, showed his own competitive fire, finishing with an equally strong 45 on the back nine. When he and his coach strode off the 18th green, they were exactly even with us for the 36-hole affair. We were moving to Sudden Death.

I banged out a great drive down the No. 1 fairway to start our playoff. Pat did the same. After Pat's second shot fell just short of the green, I hit a slashing five-iron as good as could be hit, but the ball drew just slightly and fell into the bunker on the left. Uncharacteristic of Pat Browne, he sculled his chip shot over the backside. This was our opening. If I could just hit a good sand shot anywhere on the green, chances were we would win.

Spectators hushed while we set up to the ball. At age 29, this was now the most important shot of my life. I thought of the embarrassment of my red face and hand with Floyd Fox. I thought of awkwardly falling backwards into a sand trap in front of the doctors. And I thought of my dad, who, after my devastating car accident, had literally pulled me back into the game.

I hesitated over the ball until Stuart could back up out of the way. "Okay," he whispered. *Shwoosh-tshshsh.* The crowd standing around the green let out a yell. The ball had flown up out of the sand, and run just ten feet beyond the hole. We babied up the putt, and got down with a glorious tap-in five. Our band of followers hollered and cheered! Smiling broadly, I reached my right hand up toward Stuart for a congratulatory high-five. "Yes, yes, yes, buddy! We prepared, we competed, and we won the National Championship!"

Now here we are today, and all of this comes so easily in the telling. It comes easily, even though it occurred more than 30 years ago. It's a memory that will, for me, always remain as vivid as if it had been yesterday. We won! But the "winning" part has long been surpassed by a deeper meaning.

Recently, here in Nashville, I sat in the audience listening to Stuart recount our Firestone experience to some 200 members of the Nashville Sports Council at an awards breakfast meeting. Standing at the speaker's podium, Stuart recounted the challenge we faced together those many years ago. "This bunker to the left of the green was ominously deep, and as always is the case in a sand trap, difficult. Still," Stuart continued, "I wasn't about to disclose to David just *how* difficult it was." Stuart said he told his player only the following, "Dave, you need to swing through the sand just a little harder than usual."

"As soon as David finished hitting that gorgeous bunker shot, I just had to let him know my little secret. Right there in the sand trap, before guiding us out, I handed David back the grip end of his sand wedge and told him to hang on. I walked him forward, and stretched the face end of the club up and out to touch the top of the trap cresting ahead of us toward the green." Stuart went on, "David's eyes opened wide when he felt that the top edge of the hazard was clearly over our heads."

"Not to get too philosophical," said Stuart, "but there is a moral here. So long as we are not intimidated by what lies ahead, we can overcome most anything."

What good is golf to anyone anyway? Golf, like other competitive events, reminds us of the fears and challenges we all face every day. Never count yourself out. Don't be intimidated by the future you cannot see. Your own championship may lie just beyond your next hazard.

# ACRES OF FAMILY

At the turn of the 20th Century, Mr. Russell H. Conwell, founder of Temple University, delivered a lecture called "Acres of Diamonds." Inspired by a story he heard in Africa while on a trip around the world in 1870, he went on to present his thesis to some 6,000 audiences worldwide over an incredible 50-year period. This former Civil War captain and lawyer-turned-minister-turned-social philanthropist hammered home a single theme: Our greatest opportunities are not always found in distant pursuits, they are often as close as our own backyards.

I didn't need a lecturer to convince me. The point was brought home by a persuasive partner – blindness. It's usually a quiet companion. But when it speaks, the message is always clear.

Several years ago, my oldest sister rented a three-story beach house on the Isle of Palms, just off the mainland of Charleston, South Carolina. Connie and I, our two daughters, and the families of my six younger siblings converged on this summertime haven. We were to enjoy a five-day family reunion and vacation on the sandy shore of the Atlantic.

But it turned out to be the worst family time of my life! I must admit it came as a surprise. Listening from the back deck of our beach house, I heard people shout as they ran into the surf, and then bid others to join them with screams of delight. Everyone but me fit beautifully into what was a picturesque seascape. The blue skies, colorful swimsuits, sailboats in the ocean, people lying out or sitting together on the sand under yellow and red cabanas – it all must have looked great. But for me, feelings of isolation hit hard. It was a total shock and a very rude awakening.

Why would I have such a stubborn and peevish reaction to one of the world's most beautiful settings? Think about it. How would you feel being guided down to a spot in the tumbling sea containing your frolicking family members and still not connecting with anyone except by collision? In the midst of these gorgeous surroundings, I felt lost, trapped and unhappy. Our so-called vacation presented difficulties for me at every step. I was completely dependent on others to guide me the second I set foot out of the beach house. There was no discernible path across the choppy expanse of sand between screaming voices and sleeping sunbathers. And what if I wanted to escape by walking back to the air-conditioned house? Let's just say the beach isn't very white-cane-friendly. And thus I had no choice but to ask for help, advertising openly that here in "Paradise" I had absolutely no freedom, no capability to make it anywhere on my own. Everywhere I turned, there was nothing but sand, sand and more sand – just the opposite of what I live for: smooth, straight-edged concrete – God's greatest gift to a blind man.

*From left: Emily, Connie, David and Julia*

Back in the real world, people ask, "How's your day going?" "Just another day at the beach," some people may answer. Not me. I've learned that my own ideal world is right where Russell Conwell said it would be – as close as my own backyard.

* * *

Our first child, Emily, was due in mid October. I was 30, Connie was 29. Like many first-time parents, Connie and I attended Lamaze classes one evening a week for a few months in preparation. These classes were to bring each couple, in our case mostly me, up to speed on working together as a team at the baby's delivery.

It was late afternoon on a weekday when Connie, at home by herself, knew it was time. She hastily called our friends, a couple from our neighborhood, to drive her to the hospital. I was out of reach, sitting on a bus en route home from work. By the time I got home and settled, the phone rang – it was Connie telling me of her rush to the hospital. I telephoned another neighbor to pick me up right away and take me to Vanderbilt Medical Center.

It was around 8:00 p.m. when the critical time came. Nurses rolled Connie's hospital gurney down the hall into the delivery room. As for me, I followed with the help of another nurse and was shown to a chair in the hallway just outside. I sat and reviewed my Lamaze coaching techniques. I went over each step in my mind: how to encourage Connie to breathe properly; how she should exhale fully to relax her body and relieve pain; and how to comfort her throughout the difficult final pushes of delivery. Although I had Lamaze on my mind, our obstetrician apparently didn't. I sat in the hallway for an eternity and waited for someone to come out and guide me in. The doctor strode out three times to keep me posted on Connie's progress, plus the latest stats of the final game of the 1978 World Series. The Yankees beat the Dodgers in six. I, however, failed to make a play.

The doctor finally sent his nurse out to get me late in the game. As I entered, I could hear Connie working hard, solo, on her Lamaze techniques, and doing her best to focus on quick, shallow breathing and away from the pain. All I could do was hold her hand for her final pushes. Despite my embarrassing and frustrating absence, Connie's performance through the ordeal of natural childbirth was phenomenal. Our newborn Emily, likewise, scored high – a perfect "10" on the healthy baby scale.

*With daughter Emily*

The arrival of our second daughter, Julia, followed a surprisingly similar track, but was memorable for different reasons. This time it was our homeowner's insurance agent who played an essential role. He happened to be making an annual review service call at our home. Connie suddenly interrupted their conversation with the news – she needed to get to the hospital, and fast. As though making a sale, the young man sprang into action, driving Connie to Vanderbilt, helping her get to the admissions desk, and then returning to our house to wait for me. As all of this was happening, I was again oblivious as I made my way home from work. This gracious young guy was calmly sitting on our front patio as I walked up the hill from the Belmont Boulevard bus stop. "David, it's Michael, your insurance man." Like an Archangel, he "proclaimed" the good news, totally shocking me with his unfamiliar voice as I walked into the patio.

This go-around, thankfully, I executed my Lamaze coaching responsibilities from the very start of labor and in a manner more alert to Connie's needs. But my performance, fell short of Connie's sterling efforts. Soon newborn Julia arrived – six pounds, ten ounces, contented and calm, just not all that interested in opening her eyes as yet to her new world. Yes, I improved my coaching, but what comes quickest to memory is not Julia's delivery at the hospital, but her arrival home. As we brought our lightly blanketed baby home for the first time, 2-year-old Emily made her famous pronouncement, "Well folks, the party's over!" It was an insightful quip by a precocious toddler, but little did she know, the party had just begun.

Handling diapers and baths for our baby girls came almost as naturally to me as it did to Connie. Back in my youth, my younger siblings Mary K. and Julia were soon followed by the birth of little Gloria Jane and then Jon. Mom often looked to me, as the oldest, to help with bathing and occasionally diapering.

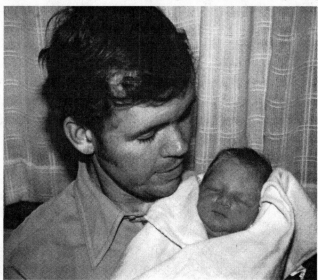

*With daughter Julia*

Like many a young child then and now, I learned early how to help with little ones. In a fun-loving, more adult manner, one of Connie's brothers-in-law, too, spoke fondly of his role helping to rear his two daughters and three sons. He always said that he got so good with babies that he could "change a diaper with one hand and eat a ham sandwich with the other." For me, it took two hands for either, but I nonetheless claimed bragging rights on both.

As the girls got a little older, I would pull them around the neighborhood in a red Western Flyer wagon. The wagon rattled over pavement as Emily, 7, and Julia, 5, sat cross-legged, one behind the other. They laughed and talked as the three of us bounced and bumped our way down the hill on the right side of our neighborhood street. People would ask if I wanted help getting us up on the safer sidewalk, but I had my reasons for keeping us down on the lower pavement. For a blind dad who would otherwise have to negotiate trees, bushes, driveway cuts and drop-off curbs, our less-cluttered street was far safer.

I remained ultra alert for the sounds of any vehicle and, by tapping my white cane down the open pavement in front of me, I was able to reach out for the bumper of any car or truck that might be parked in our path. Our travel objective? For me, it was fun quality time with my daughters. For the girls, it was candy at the neighborhood market.

Two blocks down the street at the bottom of the hill, we faced Belmont Boulevard. It was the one busy thoroughfare we had to cross to get to our destination. There was no light or stop sign at this intersection. "Quiet, girls. Dad needs to listen for traffic." I spoke these words firmly, always emphasizing the importance of safety at this critical juncture.

Twenty cars later, we got the break in traffic we were looking for. A low-pitch hum of tires faded away 100 yards to my right. A second hum of tires receded to my left. This was my reliable signal that our opening was clear. "What do you see, girls? Look safe?" I would not step forward unless their response was an unequivocal "Yes." And with that, I extended my white cane left and right as a final safeguard, and towed my precious cargo across the road.

Upon reaching the other side, happiness breathed out of us again. Now we had to get off the busy thoroughfare and up onto the sidewalk. Riding in the lap of luxury, Emily and Julia continued their chatter and laughter, with an occasional call to their dad to avoid overhanging limbs or upcoming bumps and high curb drop-offs. Soon arriving at our neighborhood Bi-Rite grocery, our roles abruptly reversed. Leaving the wagon out front, my job switched from leader to follower. In the store, we treaded up and down the aisles, with me – the parent – pulled by the hand of one daughter or the other.

Candy purchased, we resumed our wagon ride home. After another careful crossing of Belmont, we trekked up the hill to the shade of our front yard. "Now what do you wanna play, Daddy?" the girls asked, as though our just-completed downhill-uphill excursion took no effort whatsoever. Nonetheless, more often than not I would offer one of their favorites, "Girls, may I have your attention? Tennis, anyone?"

Wimbledon on the Green would be an impossibly fast-paced game for someone like me. Such a challenge would require considerable and clever adaptation. After all, how could a blind dad volley and manage returns from two wonderfully sighted daughters?

Pow! I used a tennis racket to pound the ball straight up. We all three gazed to the treetops and followed the ball back to one of the girls below. Whoever was the designated catcher would extend both hands as though begging for alms. The ball would usually be caught with a happy yelp and a laugh, landing in an upside-down golf cap, held steady by a pair of small waiting hands.

Time and time again, we returned to this vertical tennis game. My young daughters had no problem relating to a dad who could not see. As far as they knew in their early years, tennis was a game that was supposed to be played straight up. No score-keeping. We just played to a love-love tie.

When the girls were 11 and 9 they accompanied their mom and me to the United States Blind Golf Association National Championship, their first time to see a golf tournament. That year it was played in Orlando, with the delectable promise of three days at Disney World to follow.

At the course, Connie would walk somewhere to the side or behind our foursome, proudly carrying out her role as loving spectator. The girls rode with Stuart and me, standing on the back of our golf cart. The two of them were having a ball. But speaking of balls, what surprised them most was the odd behavior of competitors and spectators.

Emily and Julia could not believe their eyes and ears. They witnessed the golfers and coaches – and even some of the spectators – yell, cajole, banter, and beg for golf shots to make in-flight corrections. "Get up!" "Slow down!" "Bounce right!" "Jump that creek!" "Kick off that tree!" Every golfer and coach expected the maximum from Lady Luck. Our girls had no idea that people talked to and yelled at their golf balls. They fell to the ground with laughter.

In every way, blindness required our family to support one another. During the girls' grade school and high school years, they came downtown with me on a city bus many a Saturday morning to sort and read the week's accumulation of business mail. I like to think this work helped them along the way, but in any case, it's what was needed to keep us afloat. Over the years, our daughters have grown up to be independent and complex young women with a well-earned character trait called *perspective*.

Emily eventually married and brought two terrific grandchildren into our lives. But would these grandchildren adapt to their grandfather like our own children did?

The first time I held Emily's first newborn, James, in my arms, I told Connie and Emily that he was built like a second baseman. I never played much baseball, but he just struck me that way. He could lift his head, and he was well-built, compact, and ready to run. The little guy had so much going for him!

The months flew as our little grandson grew in experience and size. At age two Jamey was already extremely mobile for his age. I sat in the den with him as he quickly toddled over to a stack of videotapes sitting on the fireplace hearth just a few feet away. "Gandad. What this?" He wanted me to read the label. Kneeling down to the floor with him, I figured this would be a good time to connect with my grandson on an important topic. Taking the video in one hand and Jamey's little shoulder in the other, I focused his attention. "Jamey, listen." I rattled the video on the carpet, and drew an imaginary line from my eyes down to the box. "Jamey," I said, "Grandad cannot see those words." He looked up. "Why, Gandad?"

Okay, I had his attention and my chance to break through. I searched for the right answer. "Well, Jamey," I began, "Grandad cannot see those words because... well, because Grandad's eyes are broken." I suppose I hoped a discussion would follow. Instead, he simply ignored me and crawled away to chase marbles across our kitchen floor.

We did not see Jamey again until the next Sunday morning at church. Just prior to the service, Emily walked our way. She let Jamey enter the pew where Connie and I were sitting. Jamey climbed up on the kneeler, and then to a standing position on my lap. Pressing his little hands to the outside corners of my eyes, he leaned his face close to mine, and asked, "Gandad, eyes still boken?" *Wow! The little man remembered after all!* I smiled broadly, and felt as proud as any grandparent ever could. My eyes were broken all right, but I saw all I needed to see – I saw one more diamond in our own backyard.

*From left: Connie, David, James, Scotty, Emily, Charlotte, and Julia, 2002*

*From left: David, James, Charlotte, and Connie, 2009*

# CHAPTER 12

# SELLING LIFE INSURANCE

As soon as I stepped into the Northwestern Mutual building in the summer of 1982, I felt I had come to the right place. Air conditioning offered relief from the summer heat. Wall-to-wall carpeting welcomed me down the hallway and softened the noise from outside. The quiet interior conveyed money, much more so than the hard echoes bouncing around the halls of City Government, my employer of nearly six years. This three-story renovated building, originally built in 1905 and known as the Ambrose Building – in contrast to the public sector, was not reverberating with the loud bustle of a petitioning public. The sound was one of rich, deliberate silence.

Hesitating a few seconds to listen, I reached some preliminary conclusions. *Surely this interior must be appealing to the eye, with art hanging on textured walls, offset doorways to offices, and perhaps a few well-placed furniture pieces to welcome invited clientele.* I began to give myself some coaching. *Just walk slowly. Stay in control. Don't knock anything over.*

I heard lubricated sounds of an elevator beckon a short distance ahead. Pushing my white cane in front of me, and ambling several paces up the hallway, I noticed with the touch of my left hand, that the textured wall rounded gracefully to my left. As I peeled off in that direction, reminiscent of my rehab facility of years ago, an older gentleman asked in a polite but direct manner what floor I was seeking. He offered to hit the correct button for me, wished me a good day, and stepped briskly on his way. At 34, I was seeking another career change, but this time already feeling comfortable in what seemed like familiar surroundings.

"So you say you want to sell," said Northwestern's managing partner, Mr. William S. Cochran. This was the man I had come to see by appointment. "Well, David, based on what you have done and told me today, I think you might have a chance."

*Man, oh, man*, I thought to myself, *I like what I'm hearing!* It wasn't that I didn't see a future for myself with the Nashville city government. I had made wonderful friends there, and believed I was making a solid contribution. But somewhere in my subconscious lingered the promise of the "Big Dream." It was time for me to pursue those Earl Nightingale motivational ideas I used to listen to with my dad. I wanted to become a moving part in the machinery of commerce and industry. I wanted to become someone I wasn't. Deep down, I still wanted to see.

After two more follow-up interviews with Northwestern, including the required talk with a staff psychologist, I got the job! Mr. Cochran had warned me this job would not be easy, and I knew he was right. And yet, still, I felt as though I was flying in the clouds, looking over all kinds of opportunities across the landscape below. I would essentially be in business within an outstanding agency of fellow professionals, each carrying his or her own weight by productivity and performance. I felt truly proud of myself for just being there. And yes, only the sky provided the limit.

I convinced myself I was hired in spite of my disability, and without inordinate concern on my employer's part about it. After working professionally for five years in Chicago and now six in Nashville, I believed I earned the job on my own merits and was hired for the right reasons. I knew that I was a qualified and determined candidate with a desire to do something not just anybody can do: succeed in outside sales.

Happily, over a period of nearly twenty years, I proved to be a smart hire. This was as much to my credit as it was to the man who made the decision. Let's face it, when Mr. Cochran hired me, my name was not on any list of "Ten Most Likely to Succeed." Yet I believed from the beginning that Mr. Cochran would receive a good return on his investment. But would my clients receive a good return on theirs? That remained to be seen.

As for my friends, in the beginning they had to wonder. Those

I spoke with questioned life insurance in general, whole life insurance in particular, and worried whether I would become just another pushy salesman. It wasn't like that with Northwestern, though. The overwhelming majority of agents – 7,000 independent sales representatives across the United States – were well-educated professional men and women living a verifiable truth. Northwestern sales people and their clients evaluated and understood Northwestern Mutual products for what they are: world-class financial instruments uniquely positioned to meet inevitable needs.

I sensed all of this in my first few weeks on the job, and eventually verified it by the truest measure – the test of time. However, the difficulty I faced was not about the caliber of the sales force or the product, but about my own physical limitations and whether or not I could overcome them.

As I said earlier about my first job, working blind in a sighted world would be not just one job, but two. Just doing the work itself is a big job. But on top of that, I somehow had to continue managing the tasks involved with doing everything that others did, only blind. These challenges would intensify every aspect of my job in professional sales.

I use the word "professional" because at Northwestern the sales representative is constantly calling on highly educated and intelligent income producers – doctors, lawyers, corporate executives, business owners, and the like. Calling on such people requires a studied approach and a knowledgeable business demeanor. But when you are aware as a salesperson that you have shortcomings – like not being able to read your proposal sheets, or complete an application form, or see your prospect's face, let alone see your way out of the room – you know each sale will be a unique challenge. The question is: Which problems can you solve on your own and which must you get help from others?

How, oh, how could I believe I'd be able to walk Blindness into a suite of doctors' offices and expect to win over one of these busy men or women with a brief sales call? Why would I think I could white cane my way into a large law office and persuade a tough-minded attorney to reach into his/her desk and write a check for the first monthly premium? Why such optimism – perhaps lunacy?

The answers would not come easily. For months, even years, beyond the normal confidence-building period, my self-assuredness was pummeled and bruised at every turn. I was constantly beset with frustrations and problems, trying to be someone who perhaps I had no business being.

*Northwestern Mutual Life, 1988*

For my very first sales call in the field, I decided I would focus my aspirations on a lighter-weight prospect. I called and secured an appointment with a young man I had met at a government-sponsored seminar some weeks earlier. That was Tommy, a moderately paid computer operator at a bank.

En route to the downtown bank where Tommy worked, I walked past several office buildings and storefronts on my right. Traffic crept along on my left. I crossed one street, and eventually another, both crossings made easier by traffic lights. Soon I approached the building I was looking for. The tip of my cane clicked back and forth between the outside wall of the bank building on my right and the sidewalk in front of me. Like a walking metronome, I moved along the front of the bank at a medium-fast tick-tock pace. The entrance waited for me just ten paces ahead.

Once in the building and safely upstairs, with the help of a few passers-by, Tommy responded comfortably when I requested, "Let me take your arm." I took Tommy's left elbow with my right hand. My young prospect guided me to a nearby empty room, the department's break room actually, and told me "At the end of the day like this, we shouldn't be interrupted here. We should be okay." Once seated, I started the meeting by explaining how we normally work.

"Tommy, allow me to introduce the process. Today I would like to ask you a few questions. These questions are to help me discover and understand your financial goals and objectives." I hesitated a second to be sure Tommy was listening, and then went on. "Once I have this information, I will take it back to my office, analyze it, and if appropriate, return by appointment to make recommendations. Tommy, does this approach seem satisfactory to you?" He gave me his okay, and I proceeded with a memorized set of fact-finding queries I had recently learned in a new agent training session.

All went well enough until I returned to Tommy's bank for my closing interview the next day. This is the follow-up appointment where I must actually present the product I recommend, and then try to get that check. After reviewing with Tommy his financial goals and objectives, I went over the general structure of the product I was proposing. Then it came down to the most difficult part of the sales process for a new salesman like me – I had to ask for the sale.

Looking into my prospect's eyes the best I could, I asked the question I had learned in training. "Tommy, do you see any reason why you shouldn't get started on this program?" "No," he said much to my surprise, "I can't think of any reason." "Neither can I," I said in my most professional voice. *What do we do next?* We just sat there.

"Well," I said, "how much could you do?" He responded, "How much would this program here be per month?" "Let's see,"

I said, "just look here on this ledger printout, and down toward the bottom left you will see some monthly numbers." "I don't see any numbers," said Tommy. "Okay," I said, "look closer." A few seconds went by without any discovery on Tommy's part. "Tommy, hand me the ledger." I pulled the printout to my side of the desk, and for some unknown reason, looked it over myself. *What the heck was I thinking?* I recovered and quickly scooted the papers back Tommy's way, and pointed to the lower left area of the printout, and asked him to look for a section called Insurance Service Account. I went on to explain, "Tommy, this would be the section showing your monthly premium." "I don't see anything about a monthly premium," said Tommy. I replied, showing a hint of exasperation, "It's right there. Just take your time."

We went on this way for a few more minutes, much to my embarrassment for having failed to better memorize column headings and locations. "Oh yes," he finally declared, "I see the figure – $1,234." Much relieved – in fact, elated – I forged ahead. "Fantastic, Tommy, thanks. That's the figure all right. That's the annual figure, which on a monthly basis... let's see now, on a monthly basis I think it comes to about $103 a month." Hesitating for a few seconds to be sure he was following, I said, "Just $103 a month will get you started toward your insurance and long range goals."

"$103 a month? That's too much," Tommy replied.

*Where do I go from here?* "Tommy," I responded with my recent training in mind, "if we could find the right commitment level for you, would there be any other reason keeping you from getting started on this plan?" "I'm not sure," said Tommy, and so we continued to negotiate, much to Tommy's credit.

Can you imagine how many days and nights this meeting might have lasted if Tommy had asked me to go ahead and take down his health history, other application information, and then finally get the check? Fortunately for both of us, we didn't get that far. Tommy eventually saved us the time by giving me a firm, "Thanks, but no thanks."

Back at my office the following day, I received help with my problem of locating numbers and column headings. My sales assistant, a full-time staff member splitting her time between me and two other sales trainees, came up with a good idea. She would use a yellow highlighter to mark the key figures on any proposal printout I was scheduled to present.

Thinking of my stumbling performance with Tommy, I remembered the words of Mr. Thomas J. Watson, founder of IBM. Greatly admired for his business wisdom, he was asked a pointed question. "What price must a person pay to succeed in life?" Having led the development of one of the world's largest and best-known corporations, Mr. Watson answered with brevity. "If you want to increase your success rate, double your failure rate." Remembering the insightful words of the man, I could not help but articulate my faith in his dictum. "Mr. Watson, I must be on your fast-track for success. I'm failing plenty. And if failure is important, I'm getting there fast."

In time, my failures became occasional successes, and my confidence grew. I soon began selling throughout the city, county, and Middle Tennessee area. My leap to the next logical step came easy. I needed a fulltime driver. But where would I find someone reliable and affordable?

I met this wonderfully self-assured elderly man through his response to my church bulletin inquiry. "Driver Needed by David Meador. Sales Background Preferred." Mr. Austin called immediately. I asked him to stop by our home that evening. Mr. Austin was confident, brash, short, bald, barrel-chested and loud.

Using skills learned long ago in my Chicago interviewing job, I soon uncovered some strong positives about this local retiree. Mr. Austin worked many years in medical industry sales as a "detail man." This is the pharmaceutical rep of today. He informed me of his secret to calling effectively on doctors: Be brief.

He would take to each physician sales appointment an old fashioned piece of kitchenware – an egg timer. He would set his wind-up device on the doctor's desk and promise, "Doc, three minutes is all I'm going to ask." And sure enough, he would wrap up his presentation with the finality of a boxing match at the closing bell. The doctors loved his showmanship and respect for their time.

Walter Austin walked with a limp, and was always slow getting out of the car. His generous heart, however, overcame any physical deficit. But what I did not pick up in my initial interview was his limited eyesight. Driving on the Interstate, for example, I would sometimes feel a sudden zig-zag and sway of automobile equilibrium. Of course it was especially disconcerting when we would occasionally drift, and then jerk back from the shoulder.

I scheduled an evening appointment with a young couple who were already policyholders. They lived in Franklin, Tennessee, a growing community twenty miles south of Nashville. An older and more experienced agent was to meet me there. Once the evenings' trust-building and fact-finding were complete, this seasoned agent was going to generously turn these clients over to me for immediate and future sales. I was excited to develop my new relationship with these prospects, and to learn from this professional. Obviously, we needed to be on time.

As I checked my watch, I could see it wasn't going to happen. "Mr. Austin," I said. "I'm thinking we may have missed our turn." It was well past dark, and we were late. My friend and dedicated driver, still commited to egg timer precision, understandably felt the pressure. "Here's a good place to turn around," I heard him say. "There's a lighted sign out front. It's a church."

Mr. Austin turned left into the parking lot. The gravel surface we were crunching over soon changed to a soft lumpy feel and sound. "Mr. Austin, I don't think we're on the gravel any more!" My driver's eyesight turned out to be much worse at night than I had realized.

And then, there was something else – Mr. Austin's hearing. From the initial interview, I took it for granted that the hearing of an octogenarian would be less than perfect. Speaking loudly to him seemed natural. But now I was forced to reach an astonishing conclusion for a blind salesman. When you combine profound hearing loss with atrocious night vision in your driver, you know you've got trouble!

"Mr. Austin? Mr. Austin, I think we are on grass!" Not hearing me over the roar of the heater, the loud radio, and the car's engine, he kept circling left on the church lawn toward the highway. I could tell we were chewing up the wet ground under the tires of his heavy eight-cylinder 1979 black Buick.

*Crunch. Thud. Zing, zing, zing!* Our back tires spun in a frantic and bewildered fashion. In a split second it happened. The front wheels dropped sharply, causing Mr. Austin to gun the gas to keep us moving. Our rear tires squealed a high-pitched alarm. Headlights now pointed perpendicular to the highway, with the car teetering over the culvert. Mr. Austin was still not fully aware of the situation as our wheels spun and the minister sprinted out of the parsonage ready to call the police.

It's easy to remember this as a comedy of errors now that it is decades after the fact. It was not so entertaining at the time. It took a local wrecker service to pull us backward off the edge of the culvert and across the church lawn. The church parson, once he talked with Mr. Austin and saw our situation, was relieved just to see us leave.

We were 45 minutes late as we finally reached our destination. Mr. Austin put everything into *park* and *perspective* drawing on his 80-plus years of experience. "You know what, David? One hundred years from now. . . one hundred years from now, nobody will think a thing about this." I took a deep breath, and slowly reached over to open my car door. "You know something, Mr. Austin, you are right."

# CHAPTER 13

# JUST ANOTHER DAY AT THE OFFICE

I always knew that becoming a successful life insurance sales-man would be a tall mountain to climb. Observers saw me as successful, but in reality I was frequently borrowing against a line of credit or tapping into savings to pay expenses. Connie and I had many heated discussions about this. Monthly rent, office as-sistant, automobile and driver, taxis, computers, office supplies, Errors and Omissions insurance, training, travel, out-of-state li-censing fees – the number of moving parts made for a heavy fi-nancial load. But, as they say, you've got to spend money to make money. Still, a more objective advisor might have asked, "David, surely scaling your mountain is not worth draining your family's savings?" Obviously, this is as logical as it is brutally honest. But for me, there was a rationale. What else could I do? Go back to college for art history? No. I loved my job, and I knew the best opportunity to provide for my family was to stay in sales.

Ten years in the business, I finally began to see results. Though I was still too often borrowing or tapping savings, my sales production in 1992 was good enough to make the prestigious Million Dollar Roundtable, representing the top six percent of sales professionals in the life insurance industry worldwide that year. And with the help of my office assistant, Janice Morrison, I set an agency sales record of sorts, over an eleven-year period, by submitting at least one new insurance application each and every week for 572 weeks in a row. More importantly, over that span I gradually built a level of trust within several circles of highly paid professionals.

A reasonable number of well-known and respected physicians, attorneys, and business owners became substantial clients of mine. I was finally competing in a sighted world. Yes, I was climbing my much-desired mountain, but not without my share of bangs and bumps along the way.

* * *

Most people responded generously when I asked for help getting around. But others could be oblivious, as I continued to discover the hard way. One afternoon, I stood on a downtown street corner after completing a nearby sales call. It was a busy intersection. As I waited at the light, intriguing sounds approached from behind. I was sure the woman was gorgeous, probably a young lawyer or legal secretary with one of the firms in that area. The rapid *click-click-click* of her heels suggested a sleek, intelligent young woman. When she stood at my side waiting for the light, the stylish scent of her perfume told me to expect a pretty voice. My white cane clearly visible, I thought she would extend common-sense generosity. Something like, "Sir, may I show you across this street?" Instead, silence.

Just ahead of the light change, I took the initiative. "Pardon me, miss, may I walk across with you?" She posed no objection. Carrying my briefcase in my left hand, I used my right to simultaneously grasp my cane and lightly attach to this young lady's left elbow. Responding to the light, we strode together into the crosswalk.

Not wanting to assume this woman deeply welcomed my company, I asked, "Miss, would you mind if I stay alongside for the next block or two? You seem to be a good, fast walker." She blurted back, "I'm on the way to my psychiatrist."

I should have let go right there. But for some reason I was disappointed this young lady did not see me as soothing to her psyche. I decided to stay attached. We briskly stepped up on the other side. Little did I know, she had made a decision of her own. She locked in on a target ahead and just to her right.

This woman veered – no, the word is plunged. She plunged like a tailback cutting behind right tackle, stepping off the curb just inches to the right of a metal pole. This was good for her but disastrous for me as I trailed on her left elbow, a fraction of a step behind. A split second before impact, I heard a man ahead of us yell, "Look out!"

Bang! The upright sign stopped me cold with a ferocious hit to the center of my forehead. *Wang, wang, wang!* The sign reverberated above my head proclaiming: No Parking This Side.

"Oh my gosh!" my fast-moving acquaintance cried as she circled back. The light of recognition trembled in her voice. She finally understood that my white cane meant "blind" – as in, "No Can See!" I sat on the sidewalk, the tall sign gloating over me as I pressed my handkerchief to my bleeding forehead. She rushed back saying, "I am so sorry!" After a brief pause, she offered her amends. "Would you like me to show you the rest of the way?" "No thanks," I muttered.

The bangs and bumps were not about to stop. They were a fact of life. I had learned mobility techniques years earlier to prevent most mishaps, but the life of a salesman often pushed the best of these skills to the limit, and the risk/benefit ratio didn't always fall my way. Sometimes the pitfalls were unique and hard to anticipate.

I hung up the phone in my second floor office one late afternoon. Outside the window, familiar sounds rolled up the side of the building from the city street below. Rumblings as deep as bass fiddles noted slow-moving cars and buses delivering people home on the busy one-way avenue out front.

I reached under the left sleeve of my suit coat and used my thumbnail to open the crystal of my Braille watch. The bottom edge swung upward like the hood of a car. Lightly gliding my index finger along the round outer edge of the face, I searched carefully for the delicate straight line of the long hand. It pointed to a position farther around its circular racetrack than I expected. The long hand pointed to what might be considered south, southeast, and just past its shorter partner. It was 4:25 p.m. and time to go. I grabbed my white cane from behind the office door and hurried down the hall to the elevator. *Just one more sales call to end the day.*

I strode north on Fourth Avenue, carrying a small leather attaché under my left arm. My destination: an attorney prospect a few city blocks away. My free hand pushed my cane ahead, all the time tapping it left and right across the sidewalk. I walked briskly past a row of restaurants and retail shops on my right, but always with a margin of care. You had to remain alert, constantly listening for the unexpected. You never knew when a customer, short on time, might run out from behind a closed door carrying an armful of packages.

At the third intersection, Deaderick Street, cars and trucks either rushed ahead or sat idling a few short paces in front and to the left of me. I was familiar with the sounds of this broad and busy intersection, as I would often catch my homebound bus on the other side. I could hear the welcoming sound of buses jostling for position at the lineup across the street.

As the light changed, I walked ahead, as fast-moving traffic accelerated up and down the road like a rushing river just a few feet to my left. It would not be unusual to hear a car or truck turn my way, traversing the pedestrian crosswalk, cutting off my steps as he or she turned directly in front of me. I extended my cane. This was no place for subtlety. I did my best to visualize the crosswalk lines I hoped like heck I was staying within.

Once I stepped up onto the far sidewalk, I tried to keep my shoulders square and continue straight. Often, there were no touchable guides or straightedge shorelines when walking on the broad slab between street and whatever obstacles awaited. In this case, streetlamps and parking meters guarded the street on my left. Knowing that these sentries would stand their ground, I gave them their space.

I tapped my way past the concrete exterior of a multi-story building that covered most of the block. The predictable evenness of the exterior wall on my right lent both safety and direction. The only exception would be the sudden appearance of a car or truck wheeling out of the building's parking garage. This would require a quick stop, and then hopefully the go-ahead to proceed.

Barely beyond the halfway point of the block, I heard traffic on the next street ahead. Soon, I advanced into breezy open air just past my guide building on the right. The traffic now became clearly audible. I extended the cane to feel for the smooth wheelchair ramp leading, almost imperceptibly, down into the street. I cornered right, edged along, and glanced off intermittent newspaper stands and flower boxes. When I heard people scuffing up and down a long set of steps, I was pretty sure I had arrived at the tall building I was looking for.

Upon feeling a broad opening, I turned right and encountered the first step. Following my training of years earlier, I held the cane barely in front of me, dangling it down to find the face and height of each step as I climbed. At the top landing, I pushed the cane ahead of me and back to its usual angle. Once inside, I kept the cane's tip down on the cold hard tile and picked up speed. A dozen or so short strides into the building's cool inside air, I slammed on the brakes. A warning shot up my arm and into my brain. Directly in front of me gaped a crippling set of stairs going down!

I jerked to a halt. My body teetered forward. The tip of my cane touched absolutely nothing. I couldn't help but wonder whom I could blame. *What kind of architect would put an open down stairway so near the entrance?* Thank God, I was wearing firmly tied shoes. If I had not stopped on a dime, I would've fallen to a paralyzing finish.

I later understood that this staircase was guarded on three sides by a polished brass banister, but open at the front. It took a full minute before I could pull myself together and go on. Angrily, slowly, carefully, I reached out for the railing on the right. On trembling limbs, I descended to the floor below.

As I reached the bottom, I heard, to my great irritation, a room full of happy chattering voices. The man approaching me on his way up volunteered a terse explanation. "It's the employee cafeteria." I turned around on shaky legs and followed my guy's footsteps back up to the ground floor. *These people were idly waiting for their buses or rides home while I nearly killed myself making another sales call. And besides that, the building's architect seemed to have something against me. He clearly intended my first visit here to be my last. Talk about an accident waiting to happen! I pity the next distracted bloke who walks in through the building's front entrance. I just hope he's not reading a newspaper!*

Once back up on the main floor, I made my way down the open hall in front of me. I stopped when I heard the hollow creaks and groans of the building's central elevators and pressed the up button. Stepping off on the twelfth floor, I hailed a fellow human. I asked if suite 1229 might be nearby. He gladly showed me to the correct door. Within minutes, I sat in front of my lawyer prospect.

My introduction and fact-finding went well. As usual, I relied on a memorized list of questions to ask this man about his life insurance philosophy and the particulars of his financial needs. The conversational style of asking from memory rather than reading questions off a survey allowed me a great deal of flexibility. Blindness here seemed a definite asset. And as you might expect, the more professionalism I showed, the more freely my prospect expressed himself. "Maybe I do need more coverage. Maybe more of my insurance ought to be permanent instead of term. And yes, I probably should consider investing for the future." As our conversation neared its end, this man saw needs he had never been able to articulate before.

I summarized my prospect's wants, and got an agreement on what I understood to be his most pressing insurance objectives. I broached an important subject: my prospect's ability to write a check and get started on additional insurance if he saw something he liked and wanted. Happily, I received the tentative agreement I was looking for. He said he could consider committing up to $200 a month. And indeed, he was open to ideas and proposals from me. I quickly dictated a few summary notes and set our next appointment.

Elated with the relationship building of this first meeting, I began thinking. *David, it's late in the day. This man will surely give you a lift back to your office if asked.* I quickly vetoed my own idea. *David, voicing your own needs here is not right. No, I'm not going to ask. I'm not going to jeopardize our good start.*

Letting myself out of my prospect's office, I white-caned my way up the empty corridor. I stepped into the elevator and correctly guessed I was alone. The floor numbers were labeled in Braille. I pressed "one" and began my descent.

After eleven rings of the bell, the elevator slowed, then stopped with a jolt, and opened to a quiet central corridor. The absence of sound indicated the late hour of the day. Two steps out, I turned toward the reassurance of outside traffic noise. I knew I needed to favor the right-hand side of the open hallway. I wanted to avoid the lion's mouth that nearly swallowed me up about an hour ago. I pushed ahead through the heavy glass doors to the traffic rumblings on the other side.

Once outdoors, I walked forward toward the steep slope of the exterior concrete steps. Undoubtedly, I was pushing toward the traffic I had earlier left behind. But then I noticed unusual sounds. They were unmistakable – cars splashing over patches of wet pavement. Then another surprise – I smacked headlong into a heavy wire mesh fence. *What the heck?* A prison-like mesh extended well above my head. Distracted, I continued talking to myself. *Wait a minute. How in the world could a metal fence have been erected on this sidewalk just while I was in the building?*

Circling my cane across the flat, hard surface around me, I realized I was standing on smoother-than-expected cement. More self-talk: *David, you might not be on the front side of the building at all.* But how could I be hearing the traffic so clearly ahead? I hesitated. *If not outside the front entrance, then where am I?*

The answer began to take shape. When I had boarded the elevator on the twelfth floor, I was sure I pressed the button for the first floor. What I should have pressed, though, was one button lower, "G" for "Ground." Yes, I was standing at the front side of the building all right, but one story too high. I must be standing inside the building's parking garage!

I turned away from the metal fence and tried retracing my steps back to the building's entrance. But somehow I got deflected off of a parked car. I shuffled toward the front of this vehicle, stepped over a cement tire block, and extended my cane over to the inside wall. One problem: There was no inside wall. Instead, I walked farther and began hearing the echo of my white cane bouncing back at me from three directions.

Feeling hot in my suit, I made a right-face turn to get out of this sultry anteroom and conked my head on an overhead pipe. I bounced left and flailed my cane forward. It banged into a large metal object. This was so ludicrous. Here I was, knocking around inside a hot, stuffy cave and flailing my cane against what must be the building's heating and air conditioning unit. It was surely the humidity and heat that brought me to fantasize. In my imagination, the object in front of me took on the shape and feel of an elephant! The pachyderm appeared dry, dusty, and in no way moved by my presence.

I began to panic. The late time of day, 5:45 in the afternoon, suddenly trumpeted into my head. I realized that if my attaché case and I did not safari our way back to the exit door in the next fifteen minutes, a security guard might lock it automatically at 6:00.

I turned to make my way out. I stumbled beyond the parked cars and finally to the metal fence. Should I try again to find my way back to the glass doors? Should I call for help? I decided my safest course was to wait and hope that a departing driver would see me on the way out. Thank goodness it happened. I heard an automobile rounding my way. Luckily, the car was driven by a young lawyer who recognized my entrapment.

In five minutes, this young attorney dropped me off in front of the Ambrose Building. It was starting to rain, but I had just enough time to go up to the second floor and grab my umbrella. Soon, I was back at street level striding at double-speed toward the lineup of buses rumbling and waiting three blocks away.

The end of a great adventure? No, not at all, just another day at the office.

# CHAPTER 14

# THE ONE THING WE KNOW

The telephone call hit me hard. I had enjoyed my client Mark's friendship for twelve years, but now he was no longer talking, no longer moving, no longer breathing. For a few seconds, as I listened, neither was I.

The call came one evening right after Connie and I had finished dinner. It was Mark's wife, Marie, calling from their home in Seattle, where they had relocated five years prior. Marie spoke quietly on the phone. "David, Mark fought hard from his hospital bed for almost a month. He just couldn't fight any longer." I was shocked – so much so that I could barely ask her, "Marie, are you saying... that Mark is dead?"

Marie was surprised I hadn't already heard. But I myself had just recently been hospitalized for several days prior for intestinal surgery, and was now home recovering. In my absence from work, a fellow agent had filled me in on Mark's accident and resultant critical condition. Nonetheless, the reality of Mark's death caught me completely off guard. Worse yet was the legal liability, a pending lawsuit that would drastically impact Mark's family and their future.

I had met Mark nearly twenty years earlier, at a local publishing firm in Nashville. He was then only 28. The firm's president and CEO, whom I had won over as a friend and client a few months earlier, had recommended me to Mark. He told me that Mark was a leader on their sales team and a young man who might enjoy working with me on his planning. Thanks to this recommendation, Mark met with me, and he soon confided that he was in a financial position to insure his life value and begin building assets for the future.

Back at my office, my assistant and I worked hard to enter Mark's income, assets and goals into the computer to create a

Personal Planning Analysis. Later at my second meeting with Mark, he was shocked to see the value of his projected income. He understood the critical importance of insuring his income capacity for his future independence and eventual retirement. But now, thanks to the projections I had prepared and presented, he especially saw and understood the value of that income capacity for such things as college funding for his children, even though we were talking about children he did not yet have. After asking me numerous questions on the integration of life insurance into his planning, he asked what every sales professional longs to hear, "Well, David, what do we need to do to get started?"

Mark ended up buying a policy initially providing $100,000 in permanent life insurance coverage, a policy that was projected to double *twice* by the time he was 65. The following year, Mark purchased an almost identical Northwestern life contract. In a relatively short time, Mark quickly built up his insurance program to a half million in permanent protection – meaning it was expensive, but it would never go away. The annual cost would never increase and it would build cash value of substantial amounts throughout his life. Soon after this, Mark married Marie and changed the beneficiary arrangement to his new bride. Despite the reluctance of many of his co-workers to buy permanent (whole life) insurance, Mark did his own thinking and followed his best judgment. He quickly committed to the long view, and began contributing over $13,000 annually to his life insurance.

Back when I first knew Mark, his sales job yielded a healthy six-figure income, but it required him to frequently travel out-of-state. A couple of years later, he moved to Seattle and into a similar sales management position with a different company. Shortly after he moved, he called and asked me to be the keynote speaker at his new company's upcoming West Coast sales meeting, and then immediately after, to speak to his Eastern division. If ever there was a business relationship that started strong and continued strong, this was it.

When Mark and his wife were blessed with their first child, he called me from Seattle to ask if I could help him add substantially to his life insurance program. So I secured an out-of-state insurance license from the state of Washington, and immediately got the wheels turning on the purchase of $3 million of inexpensive term coverage. This coverage was temporary insurance that would get more expensive over time and terminate at age 70. Only this time, we arranged for the applicant to be an "irrevocable life insurance trust." His tax attorney had suggested making the trust the owner of the policy, thus ultimately, at Mark's future death, protecting the $3 million from estate liabilities, including estate taxes. Neither of us had any way of knowing just how fortuitous this arrangement would be.

Unprepared as I was for Marie's call, I nonetheless instantly felt empathy for her loss, and realized the extent of mine. I would never have another conversation over coffee in Mark's office. There would never be a discussion about protection and accumulation strategies. He would never again smile his confident smile at the conclusion of one of our meetings. And Mark would never join me for eighteen holes of golf, as he had done on his occasional visits back to Nashville. Mark was gone, and he wasn't coming back.

How could this have happened? Mark and Marie were driving home from a Friday evening birthday dinner, Mark behind the wheel. It was raining that night in Seattle. The streets were wet and slippery, which surely played a part. Perhaps they were going a bit fast, or maybe he took his eyes off the road for a second. I do not know.

Tragically, the unthinkable happened. Mark lost control of the car. It veered, jumped the narrow median, and skidded into the path of an oncoming vehicle. A young married couple was in the other car. The wife was killed instantly. The husband, who was driving, sustained massive brain injuries leaving him paralyzed, a condition the doctors expected to be permanent. Their infant daughter, thank God, was spared, as she had been left with grandparents for the evening.

As for Marie, miraculously, she walked away with only cuts and bruises. Mark, however, was not nearly so fortunate. He suffered a direct impact that would prove fatal. Once across the median, the crash was unavoidable. Mark had tried to swerve back to the right, and out of oncoming traffic. He took the brunt of their broadside into the oncoming car. Marie said Mark had been hospitalized in intensive care, but never regained consciousness.

As Mark's widow and I were about to conclude our long-distance conversation, my mind reeled from the news. The best I could do was try to get across what was on my mind. "Marie, this is such a tragedy. But it's good that Mark did so much to protect you and your daughters." We both knew the figure. The current total was $3.6 million, of which $3 million would be paid to the family trust tax-free.

But an avalanche of unforeseen problems would continue to pile up on Marie. The situation was more complicated than any of us could have anticipated. Family members of the couple that Mark and Marie had collided with were understandably suing for damages. Reeling from their sudden loss and recognizing their responsibilities to the future of the disabled father and his infant daughter, the injured parties did what injured parties do. They pressed for a multi-million dollar settlement.

And there was another critical twist of fate. Just prior to the crash, Mark had begun the process of working with a new agent in Seattle to change his vehicle liability coverage to another carrier. For some reason, Mark had stopped paying his car insurance before getting approval for his new coverage. Marie checked every possible lead to see if their old auto liability policy might still be in force. But after an extensive investigation, she was left with a devastating conclusion: The old liability coverage was no longer in force, and the new coverage was nowhere to be found. Marie would have to face this lawsuit without her husband, and without the help of liability insurance to pay claims.

In addition to Marie's worry and grief about her own loss, she also felt guilty that she had a part in causing so much pain for others. She wanted to justly compensate the other devastated family. They, too, had suffered incredible losses – losses that could never be regained. So in a way, she felt good to have her home and a sizable investment portfolio, a total value of $2.5 million, to leave to the other family, if that's what it took.

As for the $3 million in insurance proceeds already paid by Northwestern Mutual to the trust and its trustee, this money was legally protected from the claims of creditors. Marie would rely on this for income and eventual college funding. She and her children were assured a lifetime income, plus emergency capital if needed, to provide both daughters with all that their dad would have made possible if he had lived. But for Marie, this trust had an added benefit that comforted both her heart and her conscience. Because of this trust, she could afford to part with all of her previous assets to the benefit of the family whose lives she and Mark had so drastically changed.

I tell this story for a reason. Despite my stumbles and bumps, and perhaps because of them, my two decades of actively selling life insurance bears out a single truth that I know better than most. The one thing we know about the future is that hardly anything will turn out exactly as we expect. I, for one, could speak with authority on the subject, and to the benefit of many, I did.

# CHAPTER 15

# I'M HERE TO RESIGN

Never in a million years did I think I would quit Northwestern Mutual, but here I was, only 50 and about to do exactly that. I would soon step into the office of Managing Partner Bill Cochran to resign. As the elevator carried me up from the second to the third floor, I felt an overwhelming sense of defeat. This was the same floor I had come to eighteen years earlier to ask Mr. Cochran for the opportunity to sell.

As I walked down the hallway, I glided past familiar offices of sales reps, associates and dedicated staff. They floated backwards in my stream of fond memories, though it was I who swirled out of control toward the edge of the waterfall ahead. I would miss these friends and colleagues. And worse, my resignation would likewise result in the termination of Janice, my sales assistant. Janice was my only long-term employee, a lady who handled my numerous reading and transcription needs, plus our inside office work, completion of applications, follow-up for medical histories, and communicating with underwriters in the Milwaukee home office. She was by far my best friend in the business, a devoted assistant. And there would still be another major loss: the hundreds of client relationships I had cultivated over the years. These were friendships and commitments built on the implied promise that I would represent them over a lifetime. It was now a promise I would have to break.

How could I resign after eighteen years of selling? I didn't make this decision through soul-searching behind a desk. No. The decision was forced in the field.

"Hello, David, this is Betty Kimbrose of Mid-State Commercial Printing. Charles and Jimmy asked me to call. They'd like your help with their insurance." I had met these men three years earlier, and touched base every six months in the interim. Now they were ready to act, so I set the appointment and hung up the phone.

All right! My experience and years of study were finally paying off. These printing enterprise co-owners were now calling me instead of me calling them! I had recognized three years prior that this company represented the perfect business client. I had kept up with them, and now they were seeing me as a proven professional.

I like to think that their confidence in me was justified. Starting with my sixth year in sales, I had developed a specialized knowledge in business and business applications for life insurance. I sent off books to be tape recorded and subscribed to monthly audio newsletters. I attended business breakout sessions at Northwestern Home Office Annual Meetings, and attended meetings of the Nashville Estate Planning Council. I dictated copious notes on micro cassettes that Janice would then Braille-label and catalog according to seminar topic.

At home, Connie and I struggled with the financial needs of an active family. I would too often have to request an advance from my agency account in order to meet payroll and pay business expenses. This would leave me with a paycheck to take home, but it was always a temporary fix. I could have a reasonably good commission coming two weeks later, only to see it pay back my earlier advance. Then I would have to borrow again. I felt like I was piloting a small plane with my family aboard – proud of the accomplishment, but always aware we were running out of fuel.

It was at this juncture that we got a promising break. Northwestern was experimenting with a nationwide apprenticeship program for new agents. Bill Parsons, a close friend and mentor, had brought the apprenticeship idea to Mr. Cochran. They soon had a promising new agent named Sam in mind, and essentially assigned him to me. He would bring the advantage of eyesight. He would do our driving and provide much needed assistance with paperwork in the field. In turn, I would offer him accelerat-ed knowledge and experience. This young man – a recent college graduate with character, personality and intelligence – indeed fit the bill.

Now, on top of that, in walks this perfect opportunity. The call from the printing company promised a sizeable sale at exactly the right time. With my new apprentice, I knew I was in a position to land it.

Sam and I stopped by Mid-State Commercial Printing and picked up their current life insurance policies with another company we'd been called in to evaluate. Apparently they were concerned about the policies and their increasing costs. Of course, we found plenty that we could improve upon. Each policy showed exorbitant future costs, and beyond that, a clearly delineated termination date. We studied the legal agreement between these shareholders as well. This relatively standard document proved to be a typical buy-sell agreement. It required the surviving business owner to buy out the interest of the decedent at the decedent's death. Their current life insurance policies would provide the buy-out capital for the surviving partner, so long as either partner died in the relative near future. The greater likelihood, however, was that their term policies would become prohibitively expensive in the long run – 15 to 20 years – and thus terminate long before either business owner did.

The wisdom of using level premium permanent life insurance instead of a terminating type would be easy to convey. I would propose $1 million of protection for each man. Further, I would recommend these men use their business to pay the premium – a combined $3,334 a month. Yes, this was nearly ten times more than they were paying right now, but the advantages were overwhelming. After all, this monthly outlay would not go out the window, but would accumulate as tax-deferred cash value growth over time. No matter how few or how many years they paid, they would always have paid-up life insurance and cash value. And lastly, they would even get their money back with substantial gains if at retirement they were to sell the business and walk their separate ways.

I was elated with the clarity of my thinking. But by the 55-minute mark of our meeting with these men, my elation had turned to frustration. My prospects were offered the chance to fund their business agreement with a positive solution, but instead they were becoming increasingly resistant! I twisted in my seat next to my young apprentice, who was showing more poise than I. As I sat across from these two men, I realized I'd lost their confidence. And that was not all. Although I repeatedly pointed to the need to build life insurance that would provide the long-term payout of required cash, they refused to comprehend what I was telling them. I had apparently confused these men to such a degree that they no longer wanted to even try to understand.

Now I began to feel high blood pressure, but it wasn't my own. Elevated pressures coursed through the neck of the older and more volatile of my two prospects. He was the one who would obviously rule the day on any forthcoming decision. It came. "David," the older man said abruptly, "we're not interested."

What do you see in your imagination when you know you have atrociously raised the systolic and diastolic pressures of your prospects? I envisioned two faces that had turned purple and silently quaked with tension. And remember, these were prospects who had called *me!* My own pressures, too, climbed by the minute. Why did the older man make such an abrupt decision? It was plain as the nose on either man's face. These business owners were confused. They were angry with me for wasting their time. And apparently, they were in a place they just didn't want to be.

This loss meant more than just looking bad in front of two high-potential business prospects and my young apprentice. It represented my last hope of ever selling a big case. This wasn't the first bungled opportunity. There had been others, and recent ones at that. My ability to provide for my family was in doubt. And murkier waters lay ahead. I had no more savings or credit cards to draw upon. This failed sale meant something had to drastically change.

I somehow had to collect my dignity and get out of that meeting. In front of the two rankled business owners, I trailed out of the room on the elbow of my young apprentice. There was nothing he could say, and nothing I could add. I had tried everything I could think of to keep our sputtering airplane from going down, but down it had gone.

Obviously I had violated a cardinal sales tenet: Avoid over-sophistication. It was an easy trap to fall into. I had worked diligently to become more complete in my knowledge and approach, a sophistication needed for estate planning and business sales. But the more expert I tried to be, the more hesitant my prospects became.

Suddenly, I not only knew the truth, but felt it through and through. Even with a bright college graduate apprentice, people capable of writing the big checks were just not trusting me. Gone was my hope of helping my two prospective clients and their families. Gone was the last vestige of my authority and influence over my young apprentice. And gone too, most likely, was his own enthusiasm for the life insurance business. I had let Sam down, the agency down, and my family down for what I decided would be the very last time.

When my next commission envelope was opened, and it was more o-mission than co-mission, Connie reached her breaking point. My peers were making money, good money, but I wasn't. It was time to admit I simply didn't have the abilities necessary for the bigger sales. I had given it my best, but the truth was, I had to face the inevitable.

So there I was walking down that familiar hallway to submit my resignation. I stepped into Bill's reception area and took a seat in the outer alcove. Peggy, Bill's long-time assistant, scooted out from behind her desk, opened Bill's door, and went in. Soon, she returned. "David," she announced, "come on in, Mr. Cochran's looking forward to the visit."

I'm sure my face showed something other than glowing self-confidence. Warmly greeting me as he stepped forward to guide me to a chair, I vaguely heard Bill's usual upbeat welcome. But his tone of voice quickly changed when he realized something was wrong. "Bill, I'm here to resign." Resign was a word I had long excluded from my vocabulary. It wasn't only that I imagined myself to be a "never quit" athlete from those long-ago grade school and high school days. Never in my life had I been a quitter.

But at this moment I was. At this moment, I had to be. Sometimes change is forced upon us.

Bill was silent for ten long seconds, and then asked, "Can you tell me why?" Of course, I couldn't say all I have said here. He already knew from years of private meetings with me in this office the details of my struggles. And in the past, I would always leave rejuvenated by Bill's guidance and his willingness to link me with one of the senior agents for joint work or regular coaching. There was even a time when Bill had offered to pay for golf lessons to help me regain my spirit and the National Golf Title. But by that point, I had precious little time or inclination to play golf – the pressures and demands of my day-to-day life were too consuming.

With his usual conciseness, Bill leaned forward and asked, "David, what will you do?" This was a question I had anticipated and had already talked over with Connie. I rambled on about the possibility of being hired by a certain company where a lot of my clients worked. He listened, but no doubt knew that this amounted only to speculation, without any basis in fact or the slightest commitment from anyone at that company. I stopped talking.

Silence. Bill just sat there. Then he leaned back with a sigh of deflation and sorrow. I was glad it was his turn to talk, as I had already said more than I really wanted. If there was a bright future ahead, I had no idea where.

# CHAPTER 16

## MOTIVATIONALLY SPEAKING

Finally, after hearing my frustrations with never quite making that big sale, never quite making a living, Bill spoke. "David, you've made a decision, and I will abide by it. But I have a suggestion. It's something I've been mulling over for some time." I couldn't say anything. I just listened. "David, would you talk with Connie, and let her know that I would like to explore an idea with the both of you?" He continued, "I'd like to suggest something totally different."

That very afternoon, after I'd gone home for the day, Bill's administrative assistant called to ask if we could meet with him the following morning. Connie and I were wrung out with emotion. We didn't have the energy to do anything but fold into Bill's schedule. And we were certainly curious!

The next day, Bill sat me in front of his desk and invited Connie to take the deep sofa to my right. After thanking us for coming, he explained that he understood our situation entirely. He said he felt our pain and deep bewilderment. Bill took on the role of the very best kind of management professional, asking insightful questions to clarify our personal and financial details. I must say he was masterful, showing concern that neither Connie nor I would second-guess. Here was a man who would not give up on us.

He then offered his idea. "David, I've noticed you have a skill in public speaking. I've seen this in some of our sales meetings. And I understand your recent speech at the Wisconsin Sertoma Convention was one of the best they've ever heard. David, would you be interested in developing a career in motivational speaking?"

What Bill proposed was to allow me to maintain my office and agent's contract, while receiving income from three sources. First, he offered me a modest salary as the agency's Public Relations Director. Second, I would receive monthly income from my own store of already earned renewal commissions, which were normally left to grow until retirement. Third, I would have modest loans of capital from Bill for start-up training, equipment, and marketing for my new career in public speaking. In other words, Bill was willing to financially support my transition.

I could not believe what I was hearing. Bill was coming through for me again, even though clearly I had arrived with no expectations that he could possibly offer anything more than he already had in the past. And to Connie, he opened up the chance for us to begin paying down debt and receive a consistent monthly income. I was filled with hope. Connie, tears.

Bill started this new phase of my career with a few public relations assignments, but he also wanted me to go ahead and bring him estimates on what it would cost for me to get coaching as a motivational speaker. Now, the responsibility to move forward was mine.

I immediately called a friend who connected me with the National Speakers Association local chapter president who invited me to the next meeting. In the meantime I listened to every audio book I could find on professional speaking. One of them was a speaking primer by Roger Ailes, the president of Fox News. Another was written by former Ronald Reagan speechwriter Peggy Noonan. I even borrowed a complete set of Tony Robbins and Zig Ziglar tapes from one of my clients. All were excellent, each offering a terrific set of do's and don't's.

In golf, I have found that when you study or practice intensely like this, it almost always throws your game off for a while. Sadly, I learned that the same holds true for speaking when I gave my first speech under Bill's new arrangement. This debut opportunity was especially important to Bill and me because of the occasion. It was our agency's annual kickoff to support Nashville's United Way.

Fellow agents and staff were asked to arrive 30 minutes early. The executive director of United Way also came as a show of support, and, along with my colleagues, he heard one of the worst 25-minute presentations in the history of oratory. Spouting into my head were all of the pointers and postulates posed by Noonan, Zig, and Roger.

Bill and I had earlier agreed to have my first speech videotaped. At the front of the room the lectern and I were perched on a tiny platform barely large enough to accommodate my freshly polished wingtip shoes. My right foot kept slipping off the side, which did wonders for my concentration! As I stood behind the lectern, my mind attempted to stay focused on its newly memorized phrases and transitions. The camera must have framed these struggles nicely from the shoulders up.

My speech ended with some long and flowery phrasing about "this wonderful occasion and opportunity for financial commitment to United Way, at this pinnacle moment in history, as we overlook the beautiful and majestic winding Cumberland River" and so on and so on. Agency sales reps and staff assistants suppressed sighs of relief and applauded politely. They then hurried from the room to secure places across the hall for the luncheon. I understandably felt a bit defeated. I knew then that, like insurance sales, motivational speaking would not be a cakewalk.

The videotape is still comatose somewhere in the can. It was never invited out to be reviewed. "Let's just chalk this one up to experience," counseled Connie. We walked slowly and quietly by ourselves back to the office following the lunch. A heart-to-heart talk and critique would come later.

I learned one important lesson that day. Professional speaking is not just about speaking. It's about performing and connecting with your audience. It's more than communicating, it's having the ability to entertain, energize, and inspire. It takes experience in front of live audiences to perform well.

Soon I began private training sessions with professional speaking coach Tina Vanhorn and nationally known business speaker Joe Calloway. Immediately, I began to develop a more compelling style and message. Attending monthly meetings of the National Speakers Association of TN brought me fantastic opportunities to meet other aspiring speakers and to hear big-name keynoters like Patricia Fripp, Doug Stevenson, and Mark LeBlanc. And I gained experience by giving several free talks to Kiwanis, Lions, and other local service organizations.

Over the next two years, Bill's confident backing, Connie's help with marketing, and my own hard work all paid off. In various parts of the country, I spoke at a large number of state meetings of the National Association of Insurance and Financial Advisors. I flew to twenty states – California, Texas, Wisconsin, Georgia, Wyoming, Rhode Island, Connecticut, West Virginia, Florida, and several others in between.

Along the way, I learned that the speaking business is like insurance sales. You learn by performing in front of your clients, not by isolated study alone. As I spoke before state insurance meetings around the country, I discovered the source of my authority. It was my unique combination of sales, motivational speaking, and courage to forge ahead.

With Bill's help, I secured a digital directory of business prospects. I accessed these 1,000 national trade associations through a laptop computer programmed to read the information aloud. With just a few keystrokes, my laptop deciphered any words displayed on the screen and read them to me by means of a clear and rapid synthesized voice. A device that allows a blind man to read – what could be better? And so, off to work I went!

With the directory as my guide, I telephoned all of the best-sounding prospects, ultimately contacting 500. Unfortunately, only a handful got back to us with any real interest, but one of these turned out to be an extraordinary find. It was a national business group called the Financial Institutions Insurance Association. They were finalizing plans for their summer national conference of sales managers in San Francisco, and asked if I was available to serve as luncheon keynote speaker. Thrilled at the prospect, I accepted!

When I landed at San Francisco International, an employee of the airport's ground assistance crew guided me down the concourse to the baggage claim area, where I discovered that the association had sent a driver to meet me. He helped me with my luggage, which included my professional tour-sized golf bag in a rolling carry case. Together, we pulled everything along behind us as we walked out of the airport and into the warm California breeze.

*David speaking at the Northwestern Mutual Annual Meeting*

I was in no way lacking in experience with airport drivers. At our National Blind Golf Championships, blind golfers and their coaches are usually met by volunteer drivers. So I was not surprised when the gentleman addressed me by name and introduced himself in the baggage claim area. But not until we drove a mile or two, with me sitting in a spacious leather backseat, did I realize my driver was no volunteer – the association had set me up with a private limousine! I tried sitting back like a movie star. As we cruised along, the driver pointed out the Golden Gate Bridge, and in no time, we wheeled through the business district and over the city's famous steep hills. Once we were down by Fisherman's Wharf, the driver pointed out something that I had already noticed. Passing us on the right was one of San Francisco's famous cable cars, complete with ringing bell. I could not help but wish Connie were with me.

When I arrived at the hotel in the late afternoon, the conference was already underway. Once I was settled upstairs, two of the association's staff came to my room and escorted me down to meet the executive director and other attendees. Later that evening, I got a bellman to show me back to my room. No point forcing my independence and zig-zag white cane travel skills if I didn't have to. Just like in the airport, the hotel provided assistance everywhere.

I rose early the next morning and attended two of the morning sessions. Before lunch, I sat in the hotel's dining room to take advantage of a little quiet time to mentally review my presentation. Through the wall and around the corner, I could hear the late morning speaker addressing my upcoming audience. His voice droned on, and he received no audible reaction whatsoever. My confidence grew.

Following lunch, the executive director enthusiastically introduced me to the applauding audience. As he spoke, I visualized everyone in the room sitting upright at their round tables. I stepped forward and presented a distinctly different appearance from the business suits that faced me. Dressed in a stylish blue golf shirt and dark slacks, I spoke with my King Cobra golf bag and clubs on my right, and a barstool on my left. I told the crowd I use this look to go back and forth from fantasy to reality.

Beginning my presentation, I moved with deliberate slowness to place my white cane in the golf bag. At the same time, I pulled out my oversize driver and took a large step or two toward the closest table of managers. This was far more within my control than trying to fill out life insurance applications without the ability to read the printed page. It was more efficient than relying on my office assistant and a tape recorder to capture, review and memorize names and notes before every sales call. And it was certainly more fun than finding my way out of a dusty alcove in a parking garage.

I tossed the club cover on the floor, and addressed my attentive audience with a brash and boastful statement. "If I were to sponsor a meeting like this, you know what I would do? I would bring in a speaker just like me." My audience was not expecting this kind of mock arrogance from a blind man. A few chuckles could be heard around the room. The others leaned forward to catch my next move.

"You know why?" Here I got into my golf stance. "Because you people need someone who can drive home a point!" Shoulders and hips square to a phantom ball, I extended my driver and directed my aim at the table in front of me. I didn't have to draw the club back a single inch. The men and women sitting closest to me gasped and began retreating from their chairs. The rest of the audience roared with delight! Head turned to the audience, I delivered my punch line, "Am I mistaken here, or am I sensing a little nervousness?"

Holding the driver casually at my side, I introduced my opening story. "Ladies and gentlemen of the Financial Institutions Insurance Association, welcome! Welcome to the Ken Venturi Guiding Eyes Classic – the 'Masters' of Blind Golf." Mixing in my own more normal voice, I added. "It's a true story, so pretend with me for a moment. We are standing on the first tee at the Mount Kisco Country Club tucked into the rolling hills of Westchester County, New York."

Toggling back to my announcer's voice, I continued. "First on the tee, from New Orleans, Louisiana, please help us welcome, with his golf coach Gerry Barousse, current reigning Masters Champion, Mr. Pat Browne!"

My audience gave Pat a rousing ovation. I made a mock swing with my driver, imitating Pat Browne's gargantuan reach, and followed it with the sound of his club head rocketing into the ball, "Whoosh, crack! Yes, Pat's drive was a long one, 250 yards right down the middle!" Pat's gallery applauded and yelled their approval.

Sensing that this group was eager to whoop and applaud again, I resumed my big announcer voice and bellowed. "Second on the tee, from Nashville, Tennessee, with his coach Stuart Smith, please help us welcome Mr. David Meador!" My audience went wild. "Nice to have a partisan crowd," I quipped. This was not the kind of speech they were used to, and they were enjoying it to the hilt.

*Ken Venturi and David on the golf course, 1979*

Returning to my golfer's stance, I extended my driver. I mimicked my biggest possible swing to match the mighty blow of Pat Browne. "Swoosh. Crack! And I'm looking down the middle..." I said these words as I held my pose and strained my eyes toward the vicinity of Pat Browne's shot in the distance. "Only one problem," I confided to my gallery. "The ball didn't go down the middle. It went that-a-way. It bounced almost between my legs."

As the audience groaned, I explained the painful truth. "The ball kicked off the heel of the club, bounced behind me, and *hit our scorekeeper!*" More groans. "Fortunately, she wasn't hurt. We apologized profusely. But then my next shot, likewise, went astray. What felt like a great recovery shot, hit squarely and straight, actually went headlong into the trunk of a large tree and ricocheted right back up on the tee! Worse yet, it stopped just inches from my original tee position! Believe it or not, the announcer actually re-announced me. 'Okay everyone. If you can stand it, one more time, from Nashville, Tennessee, David Meador!'"

I let the laughter and applause die down. Calmly I placed my driver back into the bag, and with a dramatic change of tone, pulled out my white cane and continued, "Ladies and gentlemen I tell that little story to make a very important point. Let's face it, we all [I tapped my white cane for emphasis] have our challenges. The question is: How will we respond?"

It is a point that every audience agrees with, especially when I speak to the challenges and difficulties that face the group at hand. Of course these particular conference attendees were having a great time relating to my golf foibles. But they were also starting to see the big picture. Almost without realizing it, they were appreciating my story as a metaphor for life.

I continued developing my theme. "Without obstacles to overcome, you have no real opportunity for championship. Ironically, losing my sight, in some ways, has been one of the very best things that ever happened to me. Because of blindness, I no longer have the option to waste hours and hours watching TV. I no longer have the option to jump in a car and run down to the mall for an impulsive shopping spree. In fact, I'm probably the only man in the room who can walk straight through Home Depot and not see a single thing I want!"

I concluded my speech by saying, "You, on the other hand, have far too many options. Every place you turn there are places to go, people to see, things to do. Frankly, you see too much! If any of you feel you are overloaded with too many unimportant options, I have a suggestion for you: Let go. Do what 33 years of blindness have *forced* me to do. Get a little bit blind. Get blind to those options in your life that are no longer important – and focus on those that are!"

Elated with my stories, my supporting points, and my punch lines, the association executive ran up and congratulated me in front of his sales managers. He had to. They were giving me a standing ovation! I commented, "I must have some friends here in the room." The executive gave it his own twist, "David, you have *lots* of friends here."

I knew this crowd was a special one, and that I might not get this kind of ovation every time. But I could see that this San Francisco experience represented a breakthrough. At last I had found my motivational speaking "voice."

# CHAPTER 17

# SECOND CANCER NOT A FAIR SHOT

For more than a dozen years, Everett Davis, a retired banker, has served as my golf coach. My dear friend has given countless hours of his time for practice and tournament play. It was due to Everett's dedication that we won the Guiding Eyes Classic in 2005 and 2009. And it doesn't stop there. "Everett, can you drive me to Louisville for a speaking engagement?" Everett's typical response, "What's the date?," represents a gracious willingness to do whatever he can to help with transportation and a score of other requests.

On the first tee at the Gaylord Springs Golf Links, Everett sets me up to the ball and backs away. I avoid yanking my shot into the Cumberland River on our left and hit a good one down the middle, just not very far. Now it's Everett's turn. He normally doesn't play while coaching me, but for this particular nine-hole practice at our home course, he accepted the invitation. Everett hits a good drive. I can tell by the sound of the ball on the clubface, and the silence of this giving man standing at the front of the tee that my friend has finished his swing. He has finished with a picturesque body pose – hands high, torso facing down the target line, admiring his dream shot. He has entered that sliver of golf nirvana called peace.

Peace – it was a state of mind that Connie and I desperately needed at this newest stage of our lives, but it wasn't going to happen any time soon. Suddenly, my wife and I were looking at a long and difficult course ahead. It was what we had dreaded most, the diagnosis of a new cancer.

How could cancer have us in its grip again? I had my first colonoscopy at age 50, at the encouragement of my primary care physician. Three days after the procedure, the results arrived in the mail. Color photographs showed three white mushroom-looking polyps against the healthy red inner lining of my colon. Connie looked over the photos, amazed by their clarity, and read me the form letter accompanying the photos. It stated that pre-cancerous polyps had been removed during the exam, and that there was no sign of malignancy. "Patient is encouraged to re-test in three years." There it was. No alarm, just polyps removed, no sign of cancer. But three years later when it was time for my follow-up exam, things were different.

I remember it vividly. Like the first time, I wore one of those airy hospital gowns as I lay on my side on the hospital examining table in a floating state of sedation. Woozy as I was, I heard the doctor say, "Mr. Meador, I'll need to speak with you when you are fully awake."

Shortly after the exam, I sat fully dressed and sleepy-headed in a straight-back chair. My mind was awake, but barely. Suddenly, the doctor was standing in front of me saying, "Mr. Meador, I have some bad news. I've discovered what looks to be an area of cancer." His words woke me up in a hurry. He now had my undivided attention.

"Mr. Meador, it appears that I missed seeing one of those early polyps three years back. I'm very, very sorry. It was flat and hidden by a sharp turn. We had no trouble seeing it this time. I wish it were different."

The doctor kindly stopped talking altogether, allowing this terrible news to sink in. This was not the time to hurry on to his next patient, and he knew it. "Mr. Meador, you will need surgery on that part of the colon. I will arrange for someone to get in touch with you from the hospital right away." Beginning to worry a bit about my silence, he placed his hand on my shoulder and asked, "Are you all right?"

I answered in the affirmative, but my heart sank. I accepted the doctor's verdict gracefully and thanked him for his important finding. Yet, the mind has a way of protecting itself, even to the point of fending off the truth. The doctor's words had no sooner entered my head than they were ejected without appeal. I ushered his words out of my conscious mind like misbehaving youngsters being kicked out of a movie theater. My brain wanted nothing to do with these troublemakers.

I called a taxi to pick me up at the hospital. After a short ride back to my office, I stepped into the building and then off the elevator onto the second floor. I pushed my cane ahead as I walked down the carpeted hallway. Just beyond the security door, one that required a code for access, I stepped into the hallway that led to our office. It was by now mid-afternoon. I knew Connie would still be mailing out video packages to speaking prospects. The soft shuffling of papers in the far corner told me she was at her desk, probably head down and concentrating. I interrupted and spoke to her in as straightforward a fashion as I could.

"Connie, the doctor says I need surgery." I knew this was not the best setting to break the news, but there was no way I could avoid Connie's expectation and need to know, so I came straight to the point. "He says I might have cancer."

Both our minds railed against the C-word, Connie's soul uniting with mine and feeling the rising heat of anger within. Feelings of dismay and despair merely hinged the door to our deeper torment. Down deep, we were angry, because we had already served our time. Why would "The Big C" show back up on our doorstep, when we clearly dismissed it and forbade it from our lives after such a tough go early in our marriage?

How does one process such an overwhelmingly difficult injustice? Apparently we both needed to look for our individual means of coping. Connie stayed quiet. She needed to think. As for me, I sat down at my desk and felt around for something, anything, to pull me out of this bad dream.

In a couple of minutes, I made my way across the office to Connie's desk in the opposite corner. I could only guess what her mix of emotions must be like. "Connie," I said as I knelt down on one knee and took her hand in mine, "I'm sorry. I know this is the last thing we need right now." She squeezed my hand, but otherwise remained motionless, silent.

Three days later, Connie and I took that walk, the one we had prayed we would never take again. Just like we did years earlier, we strode down the hallway of a big city hospital, this time to resume battle with an old enemy. We found ourselves once again crossing over that invisible line between cancer-burdened and cancer-free.

The Vanderbilt-Ingram Cancer Center is one of the nation's best. It is one of just 40 centers currently certified by the National Cancer Institute as "Comprehensive." With a long history of scientific research and the training of medical students, Vanderbilt is a regionally and nationally renowned institution.

The recommended cancer surgeon was Dr. Scott Pearson. Dr. Pearson sounded smart, athletic, Southern, and 15 years younger than me. He spoke with a wonderful combination of confidence and caring. He went over the colonoscopy report and, much to our relief, gave every impression that my case was one in which surgery alone would likely clear up the matter.

The angry fire within me began to quell. *Maybe we have caught this cancer early after all. At least I'm not falling into that statistical oddity of having to endure a second lifetime wrangle with radiation and chemotherapy. Surely I will avoid those two brutes this go-around.*

So, yes, Dr. Pearson lifted our spirits with his confidence and style. But there was one caveat. His concluding sentence shook us with words that were far too meaningful. "Mr. and Mrs. Meador, please be assured that if more is needed beyond surgery, we very definitely have other treatment modalities." We shuddered at the thought.

The following week I underwent five hours of surgery. In the recovery room, I remember waking and offering thanks to Dr. Pearson and his chief resident. Happy to have completed surgery, I was feeling almost no pain.

Dr. Pearson visited me each day to check on my incision. It was the afternoon of day five in the hospital when Dr. Pearson stopped by to break the news. He said the biopsy results were in, and that he would be back momentarily to go over them. Upon his return, the doctor shared his information. "David, the biopsy shows your cancer has spread to your lymph glands." The phrase "your cancer," is, of course, a repulsive one. It has a way of asserting too much ownership, far more than anyone wants. Our surgeon paused briefly, giving us a moment to recover from what must have been for him a familiar scene: two people stunned by a diagnosis of advanced cancer. Then he continued. "I'm sorry, but this cancer was present in eleven of nineteen lymph nodes we excised from around your colon." He paused and waited for us to breathe. He then added those awful words we had hoped to avoid. "I have you scheduled to come in early next week. I want you to talk with us about chemotherapy and radiation."

Now Connie and I were looking straight into the wicked eyes of those dreaded "other modalities." Recalling the radiation and four years of chemotherapy treatments we experienced long ago, we hardly knew what to say to one another, let alone to our waiting physician. Dr. Pearson was aware of this, so he allowed us our silence, letting our sense of shock settle.

The diagnosis: Stage Three, Advanced Colorectal Cancer. Our minds reeled like spinning disk drives that refused to boot up. Dr. Pearson left us to continue his patient rounds. Connie and I sat stunned, holding hands on the hospital bed. I'm usually quick to try to put a positive spin on things. But here I couldn't find one.

Friends and family had sent a number of plants and flowers during my hospital stay. Too heavy-hearted to talk, we decided Connie should go ahead and transport all of these home before my impending discharge the following morning. Utilizing a borrowed hospital cart, she hauled two loads down to the car. She would return for me Saturday morning.

All alone, I could not help but shiver from the memory of our earlier years in Chicago struggling with cancer and its treatments. I just kept thinking about those months and months of weekend vomiting bouts. And those were just for Stage One Hodgkin's Disease. This time, I was already at Stage Three. I felt I was again rapidly floating downstream, shooting toward a steep waterfall, and anticipating the churning waters below. But this would never be just my struggle. Connie would also have to keep us from tumbling over the edge. And for her, I knew this would be a much bigger job than before.

Battling cancer 30 years earlier, we were simply a young married couple living in Chicago. This time, we were parents. Like many parents our age, we were heavily engaged in the financial challenge of helping our younger daughter Julia through college. Our older daughter Emily, who had just separated from her husband, was nearing her college graduation, and needed our help caring for her 2-year-old son and soon-to-be-born daughter.

With so much happening in our family, and everyone looking to Connie for assistance, I knew that a protracted medical struggle without hope of a cure would be wrong. There was only one comforting thought. While working at Northwestern Mutual, my first cancer had been far enough in the past that I was able to medically qualify for a substantial amount of life insurance. If my second cancer was so advanced as to leave little hope of cure, I was prepared to make a big decision. I was prepared to turn the therapy down altogether, knowing that Connie would be left with enough capital from life insurance to carry on.

Just as I reached my lowest of low moments, a long-time friend walked into my hospital room. "Hello, David." His voice was low and touched with pain, as though he was clearly aware of the critical line of thinking I had just crossed over. This man was Father James K. Mallet, our parish priest, a friend of sixteen years. As my pastor stood next to me, the emotion of my decision welled up inside me. There was no small talk. He covered one of my hands with his. He asked about me. He listened.

I told Father Mallett of the doctor's words, that my disease had already spread to the lymph system. Laying all my cards on the table, I shared with our priest my innermost thought – that I would likely refuse chemotherapy altogether. Now both of his hands rested on mine. He was a great comfort. We were each trying to control our emotions. He asked me to explain why I felt chemotherapy would not be helpful.

I told him of the long battle Connie and I had, fighting cancer during those early years of our marriage. I explained that I wasn't willing to go through another long struggle, especially if there was almost no chance of being cured. My emotional state was as low as it has ever been. I almost never cry, but here, I began crying. And so also did Father Mallett.

Through tears, Father Mallett recognized that my spirit ached with sorrow. He did not counter my emotion with the possibility of a miracle cure. He gave me permission to feel the way I did. He responded with straight talk that felt surprisingly refreshing, comforting, and cleansing.

On dying, an as yet unspoken topic, the good Father shared with me his first-hand experience. He explained that he had dealt intimately with others in the parish who were terminally ill. He assured me that, if I decided to reject chemotherapy, the very best of palliative care was available close by. Father Mallett convincingly expressed how impressed he had been with the care and management of pain extended to patients in local hospice settings.

What touched me most was his personal insight into that essential subject beyond dying. "David," he said, "In all honesty, I look forward to death." He went on. "I've had my own struggles, and I sometimes feel almost as tired as you do right now. Sometimes people imagine that when they cross over that line from this life to the next, they're going to look back into their previous life. They think maybe they will see some kind of a fun party going on in their home." The good Father continued. "Yes, they think they'll wish to God they were back having a big time at that party." He paused for a second to come up with a way of presenting this more properly.

Here stood my 62-year-old parish priest, an extraordinary, highly educated man who had mastered Latin, studied in Rome, and earned a law degree from Vanderbilt University. As he paused, we both realized the incongruity of a learned priest simplifying millennia of theological study down to a "house party." We looked at one another and laughed. We laughed together, as we held hands for dear life. We shared this special moment, laughter through tears.

On the downward slope of our laughter, Father Mallett went on. "But David, it's just not going to be that way. It's going to be so good, so wonderful on the other side of that line, that there's just no way we're going to say, 'Gosh, I wish I was back home at that party.'"

When Father left the room, I felt more prepared and more accepting of death than I ever thought possible. I believed entirely the good news that he conveyed so lovingly about the life that awaits those who leave this world in faith. I just didn't know if I was quite ready to go.

# CHAPTER 18

# DECISION

On an unseasonably warm morning in February, I asked Connie to come sit with me on our patio. Leafless hackberry trees stood tall along the left and right sides of our yard. The sun shone brightly on the cedar fence that surrounded the patio. It was in this setting that, with Connie's hand in mine, I began to tell my loving wife about my much-considered decision.

"Connie, I hope you will understand. I can never ever go the radiation and chemotherapy route again. And especially not when my chances are slim at best." My wife squeezed my hand, adding her gentle touch to a poignant moment. Tears glistened and ran down my cheeks. But the salt-tinged flow was not cleansing, or satisfying, or any of those good feelings that supposedly happen when your emotions take over. I was embarrassed, turning this into a pity party, though a pitiful situation it was.

Financially, we had a few long-term investments, but fighting a long and losing battle would drain all resources. We were already up to our necks in medical bills, but managing to stay afloat thanks to Connie's keen financial skills. She was constantly on the phone chasing down claims adjusters, pleading our case for full coverage of charges. Undergoing treatments would only make a bad situation worse.

As Connie eventually spoke, she voiced her deepest concerns by asking, "David, are you saying you don't want any treatments whatsoever?" She paused, saying no more, as her question said so much already. "Connie," I said, a little irritated she was asking me to clarify my stance, "Don't you remember how awful it was all those years ago?" No doubt she did, but I kept on talking, blindly, not giving my wife the chance to answer. "I don't want to put either of us through that again. And remember - everything we agonized over or went through 30 years ago was just for a cancer caught at Stage One! And, honey," I said, bringing my tone down, "remember, this one's already Stage Three."

One often tries to deny it, but the human body has limits. Resilient, yes, but like a candle, the body has only so much fuel to burn. For me, my candle was being burned at both ends by multiple sources of heat.

For one thing, during my nearly twenty years at Northwestern Mutual, I suffered well over a dozen episodes of severe illness. These came with extreme bloating, constipation, all-night vomiting, and excruciating stomach pain. Several resulted in hurried trips to the emergency room. Four times I was hospitalized for a week or more. And two of those ended up requiring major surgeries to unbind intestines that were either tangled or blocked. Many a night, I had to bolt out of bed and to our upstairs bathroom, where I lay in agony either in the guest room or on the bathroom floor until my vomiting subsided. Why these attacks? Two major surgeries back then linked the problem to damage caused by radiation therapy for my Hodgkin's Disease years earlier in 1972. Scarring slowly but surely bound intestines together until finally, obstructions prevented their working at all. And so now, given this history, how could anyone blame me for not wanting any more?!

Sensing my fears, Connie spoke softly to me. "But David, I don't want you to..." She stopped short of saying the word. Neither of us wanted to say it. Here we were, married 32 years, in our mid 50s, and now facing the end. She cried. I cried. But in the minutes that followed, we slowly talked about our options. "David, it would not be right to reject treatments without at least checking out the facts. You owe it not just to me and our family, but to yourself."

And so, with a good deal of reluctance, I agreed to keep the appointment that my cancer surgeon, Dr. Pearson, had scheduled for me. But I made myself a promise, a promise not to be swayed by vague encouragements. *Whatever the situation, whomever the doctor, I'm going to ask for the truth about my precise chance of survival and accept the logical consequence, no matter what it may be.*

Vanderbilt Oncologist Dr. Craig Lockhart sounded quite a bit younger than Dr. Pearson. Frankly, he sounded only a year or two out of training. I questioned whether I was getting the best. Here I was trying to make a decision about whether to live or die, and it sounded like my doctor had barely any experience with either.

"Mr. Meador, if you go ahead with chemotherapy and radiation, your chance of cure is 55%." Dr. Lockhart's answer was shocking. It was authoritative and straightforward. It was as precise as my question had been to him. His answer spoke to his competence and judgment. As for my own, I now needed to re-evaluate. I knew that a 55% chance of cure wasn't enough to throw a "house party," but it certainly was enough to make me rethink things.

The day after our meeting with the oncologist, Connie offered a welcome proposal. "David, listen. I think we should take a short vacation, somewhere warm and somewhere we can get away from it all for a while. We haven't taken time for just you and me in years, and we need some time to talk." Without hesitating, I replied, "You're right, honey." I knew that Connie really needed a break too, a trip somewhere nice, a departure from our month-to-month, year-to-year routine that was embarrassingly absent of vacations. We knew it would be one of our best vacation experiences ever, and also possibly our last.

Within a few days, our trip was arranged. We were going to fly to San Diego and slowly walk long stretches of the beach. We would be there in mid-March, thus beating the rush of students on spring break. In no time, we were at the airport with bags and tickets in hand.

Unlike the family reunion of years earlier at a beach that presented me with the dichotomy of quality family time in an unfriendly environment, our simpler and quieter San Diego experience took on a much different dynamic. Walking slowly along the hissing shoreline, smelling the salty life of the ocean, and feeling the sun and breeze, Connie and I knew we were in the right place. On the second day, we sat near the water and watched the waves roll towards us, smoothing and re-smoothing a darkened runway of sand. These were the intriguing sounds that painted the particulars of my mind's eye. I embraced the close-up. Connie, meanwhile, looked to the distance. She described two sailboats far out in the bay as tiny white triangles standing motionless against a blue sky.

My mind, on the other hand, fixated on my young oncologist's proclamation of a 55% chance of cure. Meshed into the seascape of my head was a voice asking the obvious questions. *How can I have confidence in any one doctor's proclamation? How would I even know when I might be considered a winner or loser? And isn't it just as likely that treatments would fail altogether?*

Sitting in the sun, I conjured up an answer, a closing act, a clarifying vision. In a daydream state, I pictured myself in the one inevitable scene that would answer all questions. I mentally projected myself lying back in an imitation leather recliner months from now, about to take my final chemotherapy treatment. I imagined my bruised and battered arm lying flat on the armrest to my left. Straight up stretches a long plastic tube connected to a bag of chemicals dangling from an IV pole. On the partition wall in front of me hangs a dartboard. The target faces my way showing six concentric rings, half of them white, and the other half a solemn black. My nurse stands nervously nearby. "Okay, Mr. Meador, the doctor says you are finished with your treatments. It's time to test your fate. It's time to sit up and throw your dart."

For some reason, this was exactly the visual scenario my psyche needed. My odds suddenly began to look a bit more attractive, yet also somehow *not* so attractive. It would be a game of chance, but one I had to play. Now I had the image necessary to counter my earlier thinking. If my fate would just land on one of those white target rings, and avoid the black, I would survive. And there was one more positive. Much to my surprise, Dr. Lockhart estimated that my treatment regimen would last only six months. So my decision to trust the odds and go ahead with the doctor's recommendations became a non-decision. Like a newly cast engine block waiting at the start of a long and winding assembly line, I let myself be hoisted in.

The first step, chemotherapy, began just as my daydream envisioned. Every Tuesday morning, I was instructed to lie back in one of those recliners. Oddly enough, there were no darts and no dartboards. Instead, TV sets hung on the front wall of each cubicle, every patient having access to his or her favorite daytime programs. Nurses and care partners competed with the blare of soap operas, commercials, and talk shows as each tended to his or her assigned chemotherapy recipient.

My nurse walked my way and cheerfully offered a welcome surprise. In the 30 years since my chemotherapy treatments in the 1970s, fantastic progress had been made in the prevention of nausea. My nurse handed me three little pills in a small paper cup. They arrived just prior to each week's flow of medicine. Not once did I experience a vomiting bout. I hoped it was the same for my neighbors.

Despite the softening effects of modern medicines, chemotherapy treatments still took a toll. Between weekly treatments, I fainted and fell like a tree twice while at our bathroom vanity. The first time I was fortunate, as Connie was with me and eased me down with a spontaneous bear hug from behind. The second time I was alone. My head hit the wall behind me as I fell, leaving a crown-shaped dent about waist-high in the wall. Throughout this long stretch of spring, summer and fall months, fatigue dominated my every move. Sitting at the kitchen table, I never felt much like eating. I would hold my head up with my hand and stare down at a single saltine cracker as if it were a side of beef. I lost my appetite, lost most of my hair, and lost twenty pounds.

Just when I thought my exhaustion was at its worst, my doctor increased the duration and flow of chemicals. For 30 consecutive days, I carried with me 24/7 an electronic conveyance called a continuous infusion pump. About the size of a toaster, it hung by a shoulder strap and bounced heavily against my hip as I walked. Every hour of every day and night, this weighty dispenser used a nearly silent pump and a computer chip to pulse medicine into me through a gangly line of tubing. Beginning at the top of the box, the tubing snaked up the inside of my shirt and then down through my right sleeve. The tubing then had to make a U-turn at my wrist and go back up the inward side of my forearm to a flexible catheter implanted deep in the crook of my elbow. How deep? Deep enough to allow a Vanderbilt specialist to push the plastic tubing up the vein in my arm and then laterally over to my heart!

As you can imagine, there were some complications. I woke one morning caught up in a horrible tangle. Sixteen inches of bloody tubing dangled out of the crook of my arm. "How in the world...?" Overnight, a loop must have caught up under me, allowing me to yank out this bloody entrail as I turned over in my sleep. Tellingly, two ends of loose tape flapped free at the site. "There really should be no way for this to happen," I complained under my breath, wanting to blame the infusion company's technician for bungling the tape job. In an irritated phone call, I explained our situation and asked the infusion company for help. Instead of sending their usual technician, an intravenous specialist at Vanderbilt met with us at the hospital. There, carefully and meticulously, the specialist re-inserted the tubing back up my arm and across to my heart. At my stern insistence, she took extra care to re-tape and re-secure the site. This was nothing to her, but everything to me. And like a prizefighter stepping back into the ring, I would be well served by the taping.

According to treatment protocol, it was now time to again step up the fight. My doctor arranged for me to see the hospital's director of radiation therapy. One thing became clear right away. In the treatment chambers of her department, it wouldn't just be my veins taking jabs. Instead, the inner tissues of my rear end would also be the target.

If my overall treatment regimen could indeed be compared to a boxing match, the upcoming radiation would be Round Three. Earlier recliner chair chemo and continuous intravenous infusions were Rounds One and Two, both already well underway. Continuous infusion would not stop until the radiation did. For Round Three, Connie and I harbored extra fears. We knew very well that radiation can easily cause invasive scarring. But here, as before, we had no choice.

Lying face down on two fresh towels, I would be scooted by technicians an inch or two up or back or sideways to achieve perfect positioning. While one readied the machine, the other tech parted my gown and drew lines on my bare rear end with a green marker. Then came a slow electric rise toward the ceiling. On my way up, the technicians would scurry out of the room and observe through a thick pane of glass. I can't blame them for seeking protection. At the apex of my ascent, an invisible ray beamed eerily down from a Cyclops above.

I did not feel any radiation heat with these treatments, at least not initially. However, in the second half of the six weeks, a hand-size area of internal sunburn brought a growing discomfort. In that most sensitive of body regions, I suffered tremendous constipation and rawness. At home I would lie naked curled up on the floor of our shower suffering from exhaustion, needing a warm water massage. One morning my soreness was so intense, I readily agreed with Connie when she recommended we skip that day's treatment. Regardless of the risk, she made the right call.

Eventually, my six weeks of radiation came to an end. So also did my need for 24/7 chemical infusion. A technician was called to pull the tubing from my heart, down the vein in my arm, and the entire apparatus hopefully out of my life forever.

But before I could cross the finish line, I had to take a step backwards, and return to Round One: weekly chemotherapy treatments. At first, the idea of lying back in a recliner for an hour once a week offered a promise of relative calm and comfort. After all, there would be no more awkward carrying of a continuous infusion pump, and no more hard-hitting radiation. But as it turned out, my transition to presumed comfort instead offered no comfort at all. It in fact made me quite sick, sick to such a degree that I caught the eye of a not-so-casual passerby.

It was my oncologist, Dr. Lockhart, who walked through the cancer center on our first Tuesday back at chemo. He saw us out of the corner of his eye as we sat in the waiting room.

What a stroke of timing! He was surprised to see me looking so exhausted, thin, pale, and gaunt. Five months earlier, at the beginning, Dr. Lockhart had told me half-joking that his plan was to let treatments almost kill me, just not quite. Now he was concerned he might be dangerously close.

In a nearby examining room, Dr. Lockhart determined that I was extremely weak and dehydrated. Once he wrote out his medical instructions and departed, his nurse carried out his orders. She hung bags of medicines, started an IV in my arm and flipped down the light switch, leaving me tucked warm in bed as she closed the door. Cocooned under blankets and nourished by IV fluids, I slept the deepest sleep of my life.

One week later, head up and feeling alive again, I resumed my place back in the crowded chemotherapy waiting area. As usual, Connie sat alongside. We could not help but hear other conversations in the room. Bravely, these people did their best handling their illnesses, their own setbacks. One elderly man kept trying to cough into his crumpled handkerchief the stubborn sickness that was deeper than deep in his stomach. A young woman repeatedly exhaled to trigger the grind of a mechanical voice. On another day, a 15-year-old boy told his nurse he had arrived this morning from his rural West Tennessee home. The young boy said he was alone, and traveled to chemotherapy by way of a county charity van.

Seeing in my mind the struggles of my fellow patients, I began to look back, to recall how fortunate I was to have my wonderful wife, my physicians, my friends and family. It wasn't bad having my Northwestern Mutual group health insurance either. But just listening to the struggles of ordinary people thrust into drastic, life-threatening positions taught me an important lesson. How fortunate I was not to be alone.

# CHAPTER 19

# THE LAST THING I NEEDED

D r. Lockhart conveyed the good news. "Congratulations, David, your next chemotherapy treatment will be your last." As before, the doctor narrowed his comments to probabilities. "If you show no recurrence within five years, the chance of colorectal cancer ever coming back is slim." Ecstasy? No. But plenty of humble gratitude, and with good reason. When my doctor first identified my cancer as Stage Three, I had no willingness to fight. So even now, as I write this next-to-last chapter, I would never say that I beat cancer. The truth is, it beat me up one side and down the other. I just survived it, and for that I thank my loving wife and all those who cared or prayed for me, and all those working in health care past or present. It was because of these people that I could now walk back across that invisible line. To them I am eternally grateful for helping me get back on the side of good health.

Since I was still employed by Northwestern Mutual at the onset of this newest struggle, the group insurance plan granted my request for disability payments. The value of this automatic monthly income made all the difference as a means of at least paying for our basic needs. House payments and groceries were assured. But disability income alone would not cover all of our expenses.

After convalescing for a couple of weeks, I found myself almost forced to get on the phone and begin drumming up speaking opportunities. I was fortunate, indeed, to have a surprising degree of energy, or at least the desire to have it. One of my first calls was to Sharon Lankford, a local real estate company executive who was about to prove herself a very good friend. I presented to her my situation (not exactly the model method of opening a sales call), and asked if I might send her my speaking resume and references. I soon received from her an invitation to serve as the leadoff speaker for three large divisional meetings of Bob Parks Realty, the regional company she headed. These speaking engagements got me back on my feet and gave me the confidence to line up more gigs. Soon, I found myself serving as the closing speaker for the Tennessee Government Management Institute. And a few months later, I flew to Tampa, Florida to keynote a meeting of the National Federation of Independent Business, which was a pretty big deal. Several times my performance was good, sometimes only fair. I was always trying to improve, but fighting hard for energy. Enough so that my health progress began slipping backwards.

On a cold January night, an attack of severe cramping and nausea worsened by the hour. Around 11:00, my wife drove me to the emergency room. Once in the ER, Connie stood at my side and completed paperwork. "Mr. Meador, on a scale of one to ten, how would you rate your pain?" "Seven" is what I told this woman, the triage nurse in charge of prioritizing the night's incoming cases. I soon wished I had ratcheted up my estimate. We took our seats and settled in for a long wait. Long indeed. After sitting with a room full of other patients for nearly two hours, a lady across the room called my name. Connie and I made our way past sleeping knees, purses, and an occasional pair of sprawled-out legs as we walked toward the waiting voice. The nurse held open the door. Connie stepped through, with me holding on to her arm, bent over in pain.

Once inside the treatment area, we felt a sense of déjà vu. Too many times in the past had we made our way down this same corridor. As in earlier times, the kinetic energy of the medical staff flowed up and down the hallway. People carried out responsibilities with precision and confidence. Soft rubber soles squeaked across vinyl. Three or four nurses, a physician's assistant, and two doctors seemed to know one another's next urgent task without having to speak or slow down.

Though just one wall separated the treatment ward from the waiting room, the contrast between the two was striking. The only sounds among the patients in the waiting room were muffled conversations beneath the TV blare. No one out front was going anywhere. Patients sat slouched, eyes closed, faces bearing frowns. They kept their movements to a minimum, trying hard to hold sickness and pain at bay. I could easily recall those inert souls, because just a few minutes earlier I had been one of them.

By this late hour, Connie was exhausted, and no doubt tired of guiding me through another episode, one more in a long string. We were more than halfway down the corridor when the nurse detoured us over to a standing upright scale. She took my word for my height, five foot eleven, and wrote down the electronic display of weight, 177 pounds. Our nurse then walked us to a small examining room where she showed us our seats, and then swiveled her attention to me. First wrapping my arm with an inflatable cuff, she took my blood pressure, then my temperature, and placed her fingers on my pulse. Once vital signs were entered into the computer, the nurse left and we settled in for what we assumed would be a long wait for the doctor. I prayed over and over again for relief from a belly that felt as big as a soccer ball.

Sooner than expected, a doctor walked in. He had me lay back on the examining table while he listened with his stethoscope pressed to my abdomen. He very quickly had a hospital employee push me in a wheelchair down the hall to X-ray. Through swirls and shadows, the X-ray confirmed the doctor's suspicion. Unfortunately, it was not the first time we had to hear these words, "Mr. Meador, your belly is wrenched tight by an intestinal blockage. We are admitting you to the hospital. But for the present, you'll be staying with us here in the ER until a room upstairs becomes available."

"My gosh, here we go again," I quietly muttered to Connie. "I know," she answered. The nurse got us settled into a holding room down the hallway and handed me a hospital gown, complete with its usual backside exposure. Connie helped me manage the ties and get into bed. Now we rested in silence, my wife sitting in a chair and me propped up on a pillow. There was nothing else to do, nothing else to say.

What the doctor didn't mention was an unwelcome procedure he had just authorized, a nasogastric (NG) tube, a proven device for immediate relief. I got word of it when the nurse carried it into my room. The NG tubing was made of semi-flexible plastic some 30 inches in length. Its purpose: to be pushed up my nose, down my esophagus, and into my stomach. There, the dangling tube would do its lowly job, gradually suctioning out my stomach's contents.

"Mr. Meador, your doctor ordered this for you. The insertion of the tubing is always uncomfortable, but I'm sure we can get through it quickly." The nurse asked if I was familiar with this procedure from past visits, which of course I was. She then handed me a small cup of water and began her standard instructions.

"I'll need you to take a drink from this cup. Swallow only when I tell you. And when I do, the trick will be to keep it up."

Having tolerated several earlier hospitalizations with this elongated soda straw down my gullet, I knew the routine for getting it there. But that didn't make it any easier. My nurse suggested that I rest my head back on the pillow, chin pointed toward the ceiling. As I did so, she inserted the lubricated tip of the tubing.

Pressing the semi-flexible plastic through my right nostril and against the very back of my nasal cavity, she calmly executed her plan. "Please swallow, Mr. Meador. Swallow again." On the third try, the tubing finally overpowered the spongy tissue resistance it encountered and forced its way down. I gagged uncontrollably, and could no longer hold back.

Rolling to the open side of my bed, I heard Connie scramble to my side. She pushed a shallow plastic emesis pan just beneath my mouth and tight to the sheet. Typical of cancer in general, it felt like more than we could handle.

Once back under control, we were promptly moved to a more accommodating holding room where Connie and I could catch a little sleep before night's end. No sooner asleep, it seemed, I woke to hear a growing stir of activity and voices out in the hallway. The commotion gave me a familiar clue. Nurses spoke clearly, briefing or being briefed, as their shift change identified the start of another day. As if on cue, our exhausted night nurse soon stepped in with a hospital worker trailing behind. "Mr. Meador we've got a room for you now up on the surgery floor." The transport person unlocked the wheels of my bed, pushed me out into the hallway, and then towards the elevator, NG tube and all. At last, I was graduating to a private room. There was no telling what might come next. But one thing was for sure – soup, salad and a sandwich would *not* be on the menu anytime soon.

CHAPTER 20

# THE MIRACLE OF BROKEN

My hospitalization that January night turned into a lengthy stay like those back in the 1980s and 90s. Thankfully, no surgery this go-around. The doctors used a continuous intravenous flow to saturate my digestive tract and free the intestinal obstruction. But by early spring, I had suffered through three more severe attacks at home. Somewhere, something had to give.

In early May, Connie drove me to Vanderbilt for a hastily arranged appointment. My attending physician back in January, cancer surgeon Dr. Ingrid Meszoely, again reviewed my history of recurring intestinal problems, and recommended surgery. In a matter of days, I was wheeled into the Operating Room and in the blink of an eye, my newest intestinal operation was over. I awoke afterwards in a semi-conscious state.

Connie's voice was the first I heard. She held my hand and stood as close to my bed as possible among multiple IV poles, drainage tubes, and even a hard plastic breathing tube that had been jammed down my throat. She bent close and spoke in clear sentences. "David, it's 5:00 on Tuesday morning. Your surgery lasted fourteen hours." *Did she say fourteen?* I wanted to ask this out loud, but the breathing tube prevented it. Unaware of my panicky distraction, Connie continued.

"Dr. Meszoely had to perform an ileostomy. It's a re-routing of your small intestine. So for now, a plastic pouch will catch waste from the right side of your belly." Pouch? Right side? I believed I understood, but was confused, still feeling the effects of general anesthesia. I was also busy fighting my growing frustration, wanting to breathe more freely, but feeling smothered by the unyielding circumference of the breathing tube.

"David, the doctor says your lower colon and surrounding

tissues were once again fused together by a web of adhesions. Re-routing your small intestine will give the damaged colon the time it needs to rest and heal." I listened but could not answer. I could only squeeze Connie's hand and nod. "Don't worry, Dr. Meszoely assures me the ileostomy is temporary." Temporary sounded good to me. And so also did the nurse's welcome news, "Mr. Meador, the doctor says it's OK to remove your breathing tube now."

After three long days and nights of round-the-clock monitoring and maintenance, I heard an especially welcome voice other than Connie's. It was the voice of my surgeon as she walked my way late on a Friday afternoon. This had surely been an exhausting week for her. I too was exhausted but ecstatic to see my doctor, my breathing tube long gone and knowing that nothing but blue skies lay ahead.

Glancing over notes on a clipboard, Dr. Meszoely asked how I was feeling. "Not too bad," I said. She then went on to expand upon what Connie had alluded to earlier. "Mr. Meador, this re-routing will give your battered colon the time it needs to heal. But in the meantime, your ostomy will require considerable hands-on management. I'll have one of the hospital's ostomy nurses stop by to give you some instruction on Monday." I interrupted. "Doctor, a question here. Are we sure that the ileostomy will be temporary?"

Dr. Meszoely hesitated. "I hope so," answered the doctor with less conviction than I wanted. "If all goes well, this should be something we can take down in six to eight weeks." But then came the extra gravity wrapped up in my surgeon's parting comment. "Mr. Meador, what I can tell you for sure is: *That* was difficult surgery."

I hoped that my exhausted doctor was able to go home for the weekend. As for me, no way. I stayed in the hospital, body sore, exhausted, and just two years short of 60. This home management thing, I knew, was going to be big. It would have to be, as the nurses emptied my pouch about every three hours. I knew I would soon be handling these frequent emptyings on my own. But every-other-day replacements of the pouch, and periodically the entire apparatus, would require help. Sorry to say, this would almost certainly call for hands-on assistance from Connie. Wishing to handle these maintenance jobs solo, I began to investigate the apparatus stuck to my belly.

Feeling the hand-size plastic pouch, my fingers explored the outer edges. I started at the pouch's uppermost quadrant, just above my belt-line, and continued tracking down to the horizontal barrette-type clip eight inches below. Under the top portion of the pouch, a hard plastic flat circular ring, about two inches in diameter, surrounded and protected the small hole in my belly. The flat ring's grooved edge snapped onto a slightly larger plastic diameter connected to a square base stuck to my abdomen.

At the center of the plastic ring lay the opening itself, known as the stoma. The small opening poked above the skin so slightly that it was barely discernible to the touch through the plastic pouch. Still, the stoma felt tender, very much like the opening of a living intestine, which is precisely what it was. But as the pouch had to be changed every other day and the underlying apparatus replaced once a week, I realized these jobs were more than I could handle on my own. Why? Let's just say, it's complicated.

Once back at home, the special training we received from the ostomy nurses proved essential. On the three mornings designated for pouch or wafer replacements each week, I would lie on the edge of our bed with Connie sitting in a chair at my side. The first two change sessions, generally Tuesday and Thursday mornings, were the easiest. Connie would remove the used pouch, clean the underlying ring and stoma, and snap a replacement pouch down onto the wafer. On the third session of each week, often Sunday morning, my courageous wife would change the entire apparatus. This would amount to removing the pouch, its connecting ring and underlying wafer, then cleaning and medicating the skin before gluing to my belly a brand new assembly. Thank God for Connie, her growing experience, patience and skill. Connie was masterful.

I told Connie, "The next car we get needs to be an ambulance." My wife didn't see the humor. And over the next several weeks, it didn't seem so funny to me either. Trips to the bathroom for pouch emptying were far too frequent. Absolute care and cleanliness was a must, which meant tons of hand washing. And talk about time consuming! Restroom visits of six or seven times a day for 20 to 30 minutes each was the norm. Thus, for both Connie and me, this temporary ostomy ruled our lives. Connie bought two months of ostomy supplies from a medical store. These implements occupied an entire shelf, both in our bathroom and in the crowded cabinetry of our emotions.

Talking with Connie, I tried rationalizing. "At least my ostomy is not visible to others." Possibly so, but it was enormously visible to me. I felt it expelling and catching gushes of fluids pumping out of me day and night. At the breakfast table, lying in bed, or sitting at my desk, there was very little predicting and no control. This was almost too much to bear, a giant biting leech clinging to my belly, and me still weak from recent surgery. And then, the occasional disaster.

Toward the end of my first week home from the hospital, we tried a new kind of pouch. It sealed with Velcro rather than the clumsy plastic clip at the bottom. Simpler to handle, yes, but, as it turned out, much easier to break free. One day, the Velcro let go as I stood up from a living room chair. Horrific odor erupted as a coffee-cup volume of warm semi-liquid rolled down my leg and onto the carpet. I yelled out for Connie. She came running. I felt humiliated. I couldn't move. I just didn't want to make the situation worse. All I could think of was to pray, "Please God, help me..." My prayer was selfish. Our plight wasn't just about me, but us.

Much to our dismay, the worst of our fears eventually came crashing down upon us. Seeing less healing of my lower colon and rectum than she wanted, Dr. Meszoely eventually asked that I submit to examinations by three specialists. Each specialist conducted examinations designed to measure rectal capacity, strength, and capability. The result: Disaster! All three specialists revealed that Dr. Meszoely's plan to rehabilitate my battered lower colon and rectum was just not working.

"Not working?" It was with the last of these three medical authorities that I asked straight out. "What are you saying, doctor? Do you mean no matter how much time we allow for healing, nothing is going to help? Nothing at all?" This man's lack of relationship with me seemed to give each of us the freedom to speak our minds. "Mr. Meador, what I am saying is, in your case, additional waiting or testing is never going to restore normal bowel function." The doctor paused, and then added a note of finality, "I'm sorry, but I do mean *never*."

My spouse and I walked slowly down the hospital corridor without speaking. Our hearts plummeted. I could not believe what we just heard. "Connie?" She didn't answer. I couldn't stand the silence. I continued, "Connie, I wonder what happened to temporary." My wife of 35 years had no comment, and could not have spoken, even if she wanted. Now we were alone and looking at a life sentence, and it was for a crime we did not commit. I couldn't help it. I'm not a violent person, but I wanted to throw a chair, kick something, or demolish a priceless sculpture with a baseball bat. But instead of the sculpture, it was I who was crumbling.

My next hospital visit with Dr. Meszoely was for the mandatory pre-operation assessment. I saw right away this would be my only chance to talk with my doctor privately and directly. I asked Connie to drive me to the hospital and drop me off at the clinic entrance. One of the curbside assistants showed me past the receptionist, and down a couple of long hallways to the busy cancer clinic. After a wait, I was called and taken back to one of the examining rooms. There, I sat on the edge of the examining table. It felt like the one that I had laid back on weeks earlier for the removal of surgical staples. Of course at this point, I harbored within me an excruciating sense of disappointment and distress. It apparently took my doctor by surprise.

Dr. Meszoely entered the little examination room and greeted me energetically. My doctor immediately glanced at some papers, no doubt my recently gathered vital signs and computer-generated profile, and took a seat just to my left. She was about to look up and ask her assessment questions when I interrupted and blurted out my own. "Dr. Meszoely, what in the world happened? What happened to your confident outlook?" I was under control, but the feelings within me were boiling up. I felt my heart racing. I spoke straight to my surgeon. "What went wrong, doctor? At first you thought the ileostomy would be taken down in six to eight weeks. Now here it is almost four months later, and nothing has turned out right. Nothing has happened like you said it would. Absolutely nothing. Nothing at all!"

Dr. Meszoely listened. She sat quietly and heard me out. Her response was as professional, intense and exact as if she were performing surgery. After a pause, she cut directly to the issue at hand. "Mr. Meador, you are right. I was overly optimistic with my first prognosis. I was too hopeful. More hopeful than I should have been."

My surgeon did not apologize. I realize now she had nothing to apologize for. She has devoted her life to serving humanity at an unbelievably busy medical center. She has used her intelligence, expertise and experience to address the complex surgical needs of men and women from all areas of the country. Her skills have been sharpened by decades of education and plenty of practice. The truth is, Dr. Meszoely focused her entire being on serving her fellow man. And so, beginning to see the bigger picture, I felt my anger subside, as I recognized a dedicated person was now being forced to face an unfortunate surgical conclusion.

The operation came quickly. Dr. Meszoely and two resident physicians closed the ileostomy opening on my belly's front right. As soon as Dr. Meszoely reconnected the previously detached small intestine back to its normal position, my surgeon and her team turned to the hardest part of the operation. They permanently closed off the lower end of the colon, and concentrated on the upper horizontal span. This is the length of the colon that transverses the abdomen from the right side to the left before turning downward to its descending path to the rectum. By concentrating on this upper portion of the large intestine, these doctors would bring the mid-section of the colon up and out of the body. The resulting outside opening, the stoma, would be the same size as before, but would reside on the belly's front left rather than front right. Known as a colostomy, this arrangement would empty waste into a pouch similar to the ileostomy. As a result, there would be no more involvement of the lower colon. No more interference by stubborn scar-tissue adhesions there. No more constipation. No more all-night vomiting episodes. But the price? This time, the tyrannical 24/7 pouch, with its underlying base glued to my belly, would be permanent! It would be forever.

* * *

At my grandson's school playground, my two small grand-children and I stood together, the three of us, under a gray sky near the end of Christmas break. At age 4, blond-haired Char-lotte walked along in her tennis shoes, long pants, shirt and new jacket. She strode anxiously across the grass and then a broad playground surface of shallow pebbles, all the time excited to be following her big brother. Jamey (now age 7 and wanting to be called James) kicked soccer-style at the brown pea-gravel just a few steps ahead of his sister. The three of us, including me sitting on the knee-high wall that held up the downward sloping hill behind, wore jackets on this breezy overcast day of 45 degrees.

Connie had dropped us off so the kids could play while she went grocery shopping. She would return in an hour to pick us up. Would it be risky leaving these young children with their blind and somewhat weakened grandfather? Perhaps. But it would just be an hour.

Both grandchildren considered themselves school age, even though little Charlotte had barely started preschool. But here, Charlotte's big brother James knew the ropes. After all, already in first grade, he was familiar with the territory. And Charlotte, too, seemed comfortable on the school grounds, so long as she was with me, or preferably tagging along with her brother.

What a good feeling, having small grandchildren looking up to you for their security. But caring for them on my own in an environment away from home was rare, and we all seemed to sense the need to be especially careful. James and his sister worked their way across the playground as I sat and listened for the tone of their every yell or joy-filled shriek.

"Grandad," Charlotte called out to me with her piercing 4-year-old voice. "Grand! Dad!" she shouted from across the playground in side-by-side syllables. "Yes," I yelled back, standing up from my seat on the stone wall.

"I... need... you." Her voice was not panicky, just beckoning, probably for a lift up onto the little kid slide or over-head horizontal ladder. "I'll be right there," I used my higher pitched voice to holler back through the breeze.

Following my cardinal rule for safety, I kept the cane's business end down near the gravel. Knowing that hard metal poles – vertical, horizontal and diagonal – lurked silently on the playground ahead, I slowed my pace and changed the position of my cane. I raised it vertically and held it at its mid-point, golf putter grip extending barely above my head, and nothing touching the ground. No longer reaching the cane out to my next step, I knew it was held upright for all the right reasons. It would protect my body from the forest of supports, monkey bars, swings, and slides between my calling granddaughter and me.

As soon as I shuffled through the pea-graveled end of the playground and heard Charlotte just beyond, I lowered the tip of my cane to the grass, tapping it forward left and right, picking up the pace. I stepped up onto a slightly elevated concrete terrace and found my way over to my little granddaughter. She stood reaching up to a pedestal water fountain near the school. She asked me to lift her and twist the knob. I tossed down my cane, lifted and held her aloft the best I could with my left arm and knee. One knee high, I used my right hand to twist the metal knob to shoot up a miniature rainbow of water for her to drink.

The next thing I knew, James threw their Frisbee into our water-filled basin. I quickly realized that Charlotte was not asking for a drink. Her brother had been using the Frisbee as a bowl to dump water on her, and now she wanted to fill the Frisbee on her own. By this point, we were all three getting soaked. I then noticed that Charlotte was no longer wearing her jacket. Growing tired and frustrated with the game, little Charlotte shivered in my arms and whimpered, "Grandad, I'm cold."

Realizing I was losing control of the situation, I put Charlotte down, picked up my cane, then hoisted her up again. Connie would be driving back to get us soon. But for me, walking across the playground with a water-soaked child in one arm and an elevated white cane in the other, presented opportunities for calamity. By tone of voice alone, I got James to gather up their jackets and lead the way.

I followed my grandson as he shuffled again across the brown pebbles. I had James walk slowly as we caravanned between playground equipment. Arriving at my little wall, I helped both kids get back into their jackets. No argument here. By now, James too was feeling cold in a stiffening breeze.

As we waited for Connie's return, James soon got the idea from Charlotte's cuddle position that he too wanted warmth up against Grandad. He snuggled up close alongside Charlotte, both on my lap as we sat on that little stone terrace, wrapped up in my jacket. It was magnificently cozy; the three of us huddled together, Grandad serving as shelter protecting them from the cold. My medical ailments suddenly seemed not so important. I knew I had plenty of life still to live, a family to love, and grandchildren to hug.

*Everett Davis and David, after winning first place at the 2009 Guiding Eyes Classic*

D avid lost his sight in a car accident at age 18. After studying Braille and learning mobility skills, David returned to college at Southern Illinois University, earning a bachelor's degree in Business Communications, and then a master's degree in Industrial Relations from Loyola University of Chicago.

In 1982, David began a 20-year sales career with Northwestern Mutual Life in Nashville. Many people felt selling insurance could not be done without sight. Despite the skeptics, David qualified for the Million Dollar Round Table and set the Nashville Agency record of 572 consecutive weeks of production—bringing in new business every week for 11 straight years.

David is a National Blind Golf Champion, a recent winner of the Masters of Blind Golf, and to date has hit three holes-in-one. He received the Kaia Jergenson Courage Award from the Nashville Sports Council in 2003. His two greatest victories, however, came in 1972 and 2002 when he beat cancer both times.

David and his wife of 39 years, Connie, live in Nashville, Tennessee. They have two grown daughters and two growing-too-quickly grandchildren.

David continues to inspire audiences through his motivational speaking.

Visit www.davidmeador.com for more information.

LaVergne, TN USA
06 December 2010
207511LV00002B/2/P